Starting a
Cake Decorating Business
from Home

Revised edition 2011

Kathy Moore

First published in March 2004; this revised edition published in March 2011 by B. Dutton Publishing Limited, The Grange, Hones Yard, Farnham, Surrey, GU9 8BB.

ISBN-13: 978-1-905113-23-1

Publisher: Beverley Dutton

Editor: Jenny Stewart

Art Director/Designer: Sarah Ryan

Deputy Editor: Jenny Royle

Designer: Zena Manicom

Sub Editor/Graphic Designer: Louise Pepé

PR and Advertising Manager: Natalie Bull

Images: Kathy Moore, Kathy Moore for Culpitt, Renshaw and Squires Kitchen

Printed in Spain

Introduction

There is no doubt that setting up my own cake decorating business from home was tremendously exciting, challenging, rewarding – and very hard work! Having had many years' experience in sugarcraft, I took advantage of an opportunity to make a career of doing something I loved. Taking the first steps, researching information, locating resources and gaining the right knowledge to plan the business was perhaps the most difficult and certainly the most exasperating part. There seemed to be no specific information for those setting up a cake decorating business from home.

Eventually, through determination and perseverance, I started trading. I had planned everything carefully, and knew where I wanted my business to lead. I researched markets, costings and pricing, clarified rules, regulations and legislation, designed stationery and logos, planned marketing and advertising and finally started baking. It was a long process, but worthwhile and successful.

Subsequently, after teaching sugarcraft for a number of years, it became increasingly evident that, whilst many people harboured the same desire to run their own business from home, they too felt there was little specific information and direction. I started to run a one-day seminar, 'Starting a Cake Decorating Business from Home', at Squires Kitchen's International School of Cake Decorating and Sugarcraft. The course proved to be extremely popular and the questions asked by students supported the need for information, not just for those able to attend the seminar but in a much wider field. By writing a book I felt I was able to extend this field. Since then I have had the joy of watching successful businesses develop and flourish, and in some expand into not one but two and three outside premises.

The first edition of this book was published in 2004, bringing together two years of research and many years of experience. Following its continued success an updated revised edition in 2007 was published with the purpose of including new legislation brought into force affecting caterers. Since then further, wide-ranging legislative changes have taken place whilst technology has allowed us to trade in new and innovative ways, opening up new markets and opportunities with even more rules, regulations and legislation!

This completely new edition is a resource specifically for those wanting to start their own business from home in today's diverse market. It provides step-by-step details on the requirements needed to comply with the latest demands of the regulatory bodies, examines in depth the specifics of costing and pricing, illustrates business planning procedures in a straightforward and logical form, and highlights the wider marketing opportunities of e-commerce and the importance of market trends. It emphasises advantages and disadvantages, risks and opportunities and provides suggestions and guidance to offer you possibly the best chance for the future success of your business in today's marketplace.

Good luck and enjoy!

Kathy.

Dedication

To my husband, Stephen – you let me live my dreams, led me forward, supported me and shared the most amazing life together. With all my love and prayers, as always.

'My God loves me,
His love will never end,
He lives within my heart
For my God loves me.'

Contents

- Why do you Want to Start your own Cake Decorating Business?

- Assessing your Skills and Qualities

- Why you will Succeed: Factors for Success

- Financial Considerations

- Personal and Home Life Changes

- Working from Home

- Business Precedents

- The Next Step

Where to Begin

Many of you will have made cakes for family and friends and harboured aspirations to establish a cake decorating business from home. The aim of this chapter is to look realistically at the practical considerations, examine the advantages and disadvantages, and reflect on the impact running a business from home may have on you and those around you. The objectives for some will be that of a full- or part-time career, whilst for others their objective will be a career to fit in around family commitments with completely flexible working hours. Some may be looking to the longer term which includes expanding the business outside of the home. Whatever the aim, the common denominators are the passion, skills, talent and experience you have as a cake decorator which will be the foundation of your business.

There is no doubt that the personal satisfaction and reward for taking up this challenge can be tremendous. There is the satisfaction of personal freedom, the choice of flexible working hours, the fulfilment of using your own skills and creativity in generating your own income, the possibility of a better work-life balance, and the pleasure of knowing you have job satisfaction and control over your own life.

However, it would be foolhardy to pretend that setting up a cake decorating business is not going to be without its challenges. Many readers will have reached the point where the new business is intended to provide a permanent source of income. To stand any chance of success, every business idea needs careful research, planning, consideration and judgement. Each step needs to be planned well in advance and assessed in full: there are no shortcuts to success. By planning methodically, taking the time needed to consider your options, having the right knowledge to make the right decisions and being realistic about your strengths and weaknesses, you will be well on the way to giving your business the chance it deserves: the chance of success.

Why do you Want to Start your Own Cake Decorating Business?

Write down your reasons for running your own business and make a list of your objectives.

Before even the first decision is made, it is important to go back to basics and record your own thoughts, ideas and plans. As every business will be different depending on family, personal and financial commitments, this helps you to focus on your intended objectives realistically, consider the options available to you, examine any areas that may limit your business ideas and identify opportunities. Only then can the decision be taken to run a business which truly reflects your own personal circumstances, and which builds in the opportunity for growth, development and success.

Assessing your Skills and Qualities

The greatest determining factors of your business are you, your skills and your character.

You are your business – from start to finish – and the need to possess (or obtain!) a wide range of personal qualities will be required. Starting with the following examples, consider to what extent each of these applies to you:

Personal qualities

Determination

Perseverance

Organisation

Understanding

Stamina

Flexibility

Motivation

Commitment

Enthusiasm

Ability to make decisions

Open-mindedness

Willingness

Self confidence

Ability to communicate

Self discipline

You will probably find that you naturally possess some of these qualities; others you will develop, and some you may never learn but simply practise when the need arises!

Why you will Succeed: Factors for Success

Possibly the three most important factors which are essential if you are to succeed are:-

- Recognising your strengths and weaknesses
- Using your skills effectively
- Knowing your markets

Strengths and weaknesses

 Record your own strengths and weakness honestly.

Target the weaknesses and set a timescale to address these areas. In some instances it may be training that is needed or in others practice. You may find it useful to reassess this list every six months or so to chart your progress. Your business will depend on your strengths in all areas of cake design and decoration, and on your skills in running a business. Increasing those strengths opens the door to greater efficiency, confidence and the opportunity to reach a wider target market.

There some things that are out of our control such as the weather, growing old or the hours in a day but there are many things that are wholly within our control: strengthening our weaknesses is just one.

Using your skills effectively: do you have the cake decorating skills to meet the market demand?

If you have been decorating cakes as a hobbyist for a number of years, you will probably have substantial skills and experience in your field. However, do you have the cake decorating skills necessary to match the needs and expectations of your customers, and of a changing market? Will your current skills limit your market potential?

Identify areas in which you feel less competent and give yourself time to practise and master those skills. The more you have to offer, the greater the range of opportunities you will be able to meet, and the likelihood of a greater financial reward.

Continuing professional development is a conscious updating of your professional knowledge and the improvement of professional competence throughout a person's working life. Keep abreast of current and possible future trends, changes in style, and market demand. Optimise your businesses opportunities. Be aware of anything that may impact on your business and use that knowledge to your advantage. Continually try to develop your own ideas, designs and style so you can be one step ahead of the rest!

Other skills you will need

Running a business on your own, i.e. as a sole trader, will necessitate involvement in all areas of your business. A number of key skills in particular that will be required are:-

- Accounting
- Marketing
- Selling
- IT skills
- Communication
- Time management

Training or refresher courses in all of the above key areas are easily accessible and readily available. New small businesses often qualify for government sponsored help and training (see page 22).

Know your markets…

Where are your markets? To whom will you sell? A successful business is dependent upon you knowing your target market intimately. Your product needs to meet market demand and there needs to be a demand for you to be able to sell. These issues are discussed in greater detail in Chapter 2: The Business Plan.

Write down who your target markets are and what their demands are likely to be. Use this information when you come to write your business plan.

….And play to your strengths

There are many benefits small cake decorating businesses can have over their larger competitors: the personal touch, specific attention to detail, the ability to go the extra mile for customers, responding quickly to market trends, knowledge of local needs, and the involvement with local communities. All this helps to give small businesses an advantage over larger competitors who may struggle to match the same demands. Use these strengths to your advantage, prepare yourself and be open to opportunities.

Financial Considerations

The Business Plan (page 26) will look at profitability. However, setting up a business will involve a certain amount of financial input during the process. Particularly in the early stages of starting up the business there may be loss of regular income and it is important to plan for this and consider how this will be managed.

Research grants or sponsorships that are available to a new, small business: contact Business Link, job centres, local authorities or high street banks, for example, for further information (see Useful Contacts, pages 106 to 107).

Personal and Home Life Changes

There is no doubt that working from home will necessitate changes to your home life and living patterns. Rooms may be needed for office space, work areas or storage and those living around you may have much less access to your time. Discuss with those involved what your new responsibilities will be and how this may affect them. Listen to all points raised and views expressed as these can be enlightening. What risks will there be? Will you cope financially? Will family privacy and lifestyle patterns be disturbed? Will living accommodation be affected or changed? Will there be a change in childcare or dependants' care responsibilities? Will dependants see a change in their daily life patterns and how will you reassure them? It is important that all involved understand, appreciate, accept and support your new venture as this will play a key role in the smooth running of your business.

Working from Home

Working at home is rapidly increasing in its extent. Realistically there are both advantages and disadvantages but nearly all of the disadvantages can be overcome. It is important to be fully aware of these to enable you to make adjustments or modifications should they be required, and to be able to run your business smoothly, professionally and successfully.

Advantages of working from home	
Cost effectiveness	No rent or purchase of premises. No excessive additional heating, lighting, rates, insurance or maintenance costs.
Travel costs	Commuting costs to and from work eliminated.
Efficient use of time and increased productivity	No commuting time to and from work. Greater productivity.
Career potential	No restrictions on career potential.
Taxation	Proportion of home costs may be treated as business expenses.
Flexible hours	Working hours to suit; schedule can fit in around a healthy life-work balance.
Independence	You make the decisions.
Job satisfaction	Uses your choice of skills.
Home help	There may be an offer of additional help from others in your household.

Disadvantages of working from home	Solution suggestions
Family interruptions	Be self disciplined and set clear boundaries for an at-home work pattern. Establish your working day and plan a work schedule. It is important to set boundaries and schedules in order that both professional and personal commitments don't collide. Be firm with family and friends and let them know when you are working and when you are not. Arrange coffee/lunch with friends only in planned breaktimes. If possible create a separate work area and ask people to respect the space accordingly.
Environmental distractions	Non-business telephone callers and visitors to the home can cause distractions. Be polite and return calls outside of your working hours or in a planned breaktime. Responding to distractions may result in you having to remake icing that has set, burnt cake bases or spoilt decorations, costing not only time but money. It is your choice whether you feel it is necessary to answer your own door. Business telephone callers: pre-arrange appointment times. Consider investing in a separate business telephone line or whether you would benefit from an answerphone or voicemail service.
Isolation	Continue with outside interests and hobbies and maintain your social life (outside of working hours!). Join a professional body which you can call on for advice or support. Contacts at other local groups/ businesses can be useful for networking, knowledge of local market trends, information about suppliers and diversifying your own ideas, as well as social events and support.
Motivation	Establish a routine, plan ahead and don't procrastinate! Plan and look forward to time off work when you can switch off mentally – brain overload is not helpful.
Neighbours	Contact neighbours and advise them of your planned venture. Allay any fears they may have such as deliveries, additional parking for visiting clients or even security issues with strangers calling.
Financial security	You will be generating your own income so plan ahead and budget carefully. Keep costs to a minimum until you become more established. Make certain you will be able to cover all necessary outgoings. If your business is seasonal, look at ways to increase productivity outside of these times.

Continued overleaf

Disadvantages of working from home	Solution suggestions
Professionalism	Clients expect a professional set-up which portrays a high standard of service, efficiency and hygiene wherever the location. Conduct telephone calls, meetings and e-commerce as in any high-standard business structure. Ensure visiting clients see the right image: plan where to receive visiting clients, have everything to hand and keep it strictly business.
Home security	Your home will be your 'showroom' to visiting clients. Restrict appointments to a designated area to maintain the privacy of your family and seclusion of your home. Ensure any confidential or sensitive information is kept secure and out of sight (see data protection, page 45). Reciprocal arrangements need to be made for information submitted by clients. Home insurance premiums may be higher, so ensure you notify your insurer.
Multi-tasking	Cake design and decoration plus everything else that running a business entails all need to be fitted into your working day. List all the tasks involved and schedule time for each. An organised schedule is essential if you are going to use your time productively. Obtain training where needed before you start your business so that you can work efficiently and don't be frightened to ask for help.
No sick pay	An incentive to keep healthy! It is often said that those working from home have less anxiety and illnesses than those who don't. However, consider business insurance to cover this eventuality.
Responsibility	The responsibility of all that is involved in running your own business may initially seem overwhelming. You will make mistakes – we all do – and the important thing is not to dwell on them but to learn from them. Take each step at a time, develop your business gradually, grow with it, be objective and remain focused. When you have done a large amount of research, planned, organised, and gained knowledge to give your business the best chance of success, be confident in knowing you have done your best.
Organisation	Diarise everything and check your schedule regularly. At the end of each work day, clear up no matter how tired you are. Starting the next day having to clean up, find tools and wash sticky equipment demotivates you and wastes time. End each day by planning the day ahead. You will relax and sleep better with the day ahead scheduled.

Business Precedents

It is important to set precedents – establish your role and define your boundaries – and essential that family and friends appreciate you are now running a business with a work schedule and deadlines to meet. It can be difficult for some to accept this so a 'pre-launch' get together or party to celebrate the launch of your business is a sensitive way to communicate this and an excellent marketing opportunity. Consider booking a venue and arranging for a local radio station or newspaper to interview you (if any images are taken be certain privacy is maintained). Have some excellent cakes on display (dummies for larger cakes) and imaginative cupcakes and cookies; hand round brochures, business cards and leaflets; circulate and network and don't forget your diary or order book. More ideas for marketing your business are given in Chapter 8.

The Next Step

If, taking everything into account, you decide that setting up a cake decorating business from home remains your objective, now is the time to start your detailed plans.

Make a list of people to invite to your event. Find the contact names at your local newspaper and radio station and remember to invite family, friends and business contacts who will help support your venture.

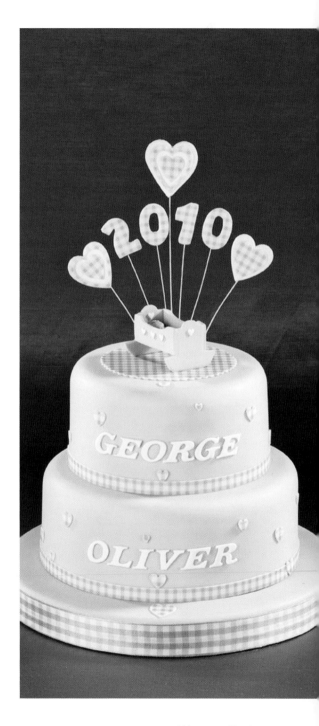

- What does a Business Plan Do?

- Writing a Business Plan

- Choosing and Using a Business Name

- Legal Status

- Description

- Objectives

- Experience, Skills and Training

- Formalities and Compliance

- Markets

- Competition and Competitor Analysis

- Marketing and Advertising

- Business Costs

- Product Costings

- Sales

- Finance

- On Completion

The Business Plan

You may feel you cannot wait to get started – that's good! However, if you are to run a successful business, planning for the future is crucial to its success, no matter how large or small your business may be. Many businesses fail because of poor planning and lack of research, so the first step you need to take to ensure that your business does not fall into this category is to create your own business plan. A sample business plan that you can work from is given at the end of this chapter.

What does a Business Plan Do?

Creating a business plan is one of the most important planning stages in any business and its usefulness should never be underestimated. It identifies:

- Where you are going.

- How you are going to get there.

- When you will get there.

Writing a Business Plan

Writing a business plan requires collecting information and bringing it together in a logical form based on your personal circumstances. It provides you with a source of data allowing you to make informed decisions about your business, chart progress, recognise weak areas, monitor financial exposure, identify opportunities, and detect potential for the future. A business plan is a powerful tool which will motivate, inspire and help you to focus on what needs to be done and when, and is part of an annual strategy for the development of your business in the future. When you have been in business for over a year, you will be able to review your performance of the previous year's trading.

- What did you do well?

- What mistakes did you make?

- Were your financial projections parallel to the results you achieved?

- Were sales in some areas better than expected and disappointing in others?

These questions will help you to identify the weaknesses in the business whilst also allowing you to build on positive results.

A good business plan needs to be:

- **Achievable**

- **Realistic**

- **Timed**

When creating a plan, the content will largely depend on the size of the business, however most business plans will include:

- Business name

- Legal status

- Description of business

- Business objectives

- Experience/skills/training

- Formalities and compliance

- Markets and competition

- Marketing and advertising

- Business costs

- Product costs

- Sales

- Finance

Choosing and Using a Business Name

Choosing a business name can be an enjoyable and creative process but one that is important to get right. An effective name is an influential marketing tool and first impressions count. It is tempting to get carried away, but being objective and choosing a name that reflects your business image and communicates your business idea can be beneficial in the short and long term. It will be used on the phone, as part of your logo, on stationery, advertising material, websites, emails and more so the right choice, to enable customers to remember you and to reach you, is vital.

Successful small business names often:

- Reflect the business you are in.

- Identify your business at first glance.

- Are timeless.

- Are easy to remember.

- Are easy to say.

- Are easy to spell.

Using names with hyphens or repeated letters may cause problems with domain name misspellings, which may make it difficult for people to find you. The same applies to quirky, unusual or purposely misspelt word forms. Abstract or overly creative names may not identify your business at first glance which is particularly important when using advertising materials (see page 92). If you are intending to create a logo, think about whether the name can be easily incorporated in graphical form.

Business names for sole traders (and partnerships)

A business name is any name under which someone conducts business other than their own name. People operating as sole traders (or partnerships) can trade under their own names, or choose a different business name. You may incorporate your entire name, or part of it, into the business name. Unless you are using only your own surname, with or without first names or initials, (e.g. Kathy Moore, K Moore, Moore) your business name will be governed by The Companies Act 2006 (**www.companieshouse.gov.uk/about/ guidance.shtml**). For instance the provisions of the Act would apply if trading as Kathy Moore Cakes but not as Kathy Moore, K Moore or Moore.

Rules and restrictions

If you decide to use a business name, there are rules and restrictions governing the choices you can make. For full details see **www. companieshouse.gov.uk/about/gbhtml/gp1. shtml#ch2**. As a sole trader a business name must not:

- Be offensive or constitute an offence.

- Include words and abbreviations that signify a particular type of business if the business is not of that type, e.g. Limited, Public Limited.

- Suggest a connection with Her Majesty's Government, any local authority or any specified public authority.

- Include sensitive words or expressions, restricted signs or punctuation.

In the main restrictions are there to prevent unfair or inappropriate trading and giving a false impression about your business.

Sensitive words apply to all types of businesses and include, for instance, Royal, Benevolent, Charity, Council, Her Majesty, Society, Trust, United Kingdom, Wales and many others. These must not be used unless you have proper entitlement. The Company and Business Names (Sensitive Words and Expressions) Regulations 2009 (**www.companieshouse.gov.uk/about/gbhtml/gp1.shtml#appA**) provide comprehensive listings and details in a clear and uncomplicated form.

You will need to check as thoroughly as possible that the name you have chosen is not being used by someone else. Correcting this could be an expensive exercise and lose potential custom if a name change is necessary.

- Check in your local Yellow Pages (or other listings), local newspapers, telephone listings and local reference library.
- Contact Companies House (see Useful Contacts Page 106).
- Check the National Business Register LLP (see Useful Contacts Page 107).
- Seek advice from Business Link (see Useful Contacts Page 106).
- Check whether your name may be similar to a trademark at **www.ipo.gov.uk/home.html**.
- Use internet search engines.

Registering your business name

As a sole trader working from home there is no requirement to register your business name,

although you may do so voluntarily to protect your business name.

Displaying your business name

If you are a sole trader (or partnership) you need to display your name, business name and address wherever you conduct business or deal with customers and suppliers (see Companies Act 2006).

If your business has a website, you need to display your business name, address and email address (see Chapter 9: Websites and E-commerce).

Displaying your business name on stationery

If you use a business name, you must include your name, business name and address on company stationery. This information needs to be printed in legible characters on all:

- Business letters
- Invoices and receipts
- Written requests for payment
- Written orders for goods or services
- Business emails

If you are in any doubt, seek further advice from Business Link or Companies House as it is an offence not to disclose your business details as required. More advice on creating business stationery can be seen in Chapter 5.

Legal Status

Legal status means the legal form of business under which you operate, e.g. sole trader, partnership, limited liability partnership or limited company.

Sole trader tends to be the most popular and easiest way for a small business owner to start up and is the choice of nearly all those starting up a cake decorating business from home. Information about this is outlined below together with brief details on how this compares to partnership status.

Sole Trader	Partnership
This is defined as a business where one person runs and is legally responsible for the business. This is by far the least complicated and most common status for those starting a cake decorating business from home. When you operate as a sole trader it means that:	This is defined as two or more people (up to 20) trading together as a single business. If you operate as a partnership it means that:
You have total control and responsibility for all aspects of your business.	Partners usually share the responsibility for running the business.
You are solely responsible for any business debts incurred and any liabilities.	You are liable for your own and your partner's business debts.
You are required to pay your own National Insurance contributions (see Tax and National Insurance on page 42 or **www.hmrc.gov.uk**).	Each partner pays their own National Insurance contributions (see **www.hmrc.gov.uk**).
Your profits are taxed as personal income.	Each partner pays their own income tax based on their share of the profits.
You receive all the profits. You make all the decisions.	A formal partnership agreement covering the responsibilities and rights of each partner should be drawn up by a solicitor. This can also provide details on how the profits will be shared.
You do not need to register your business name.	You do not need to register the business name.

Description

Record in full details of your products, services and intentions. It is a shrewd move to review this on a regular basis, in particular, as a comparison to your competitors.

Objectives

First and foremost you need to consider your business objectives but try also to set personal objectives and build these into your overall plan. Objectives need to be realistic, achievable and timed. Not setting a timeframe means wandering aimlessly, never knowing when you will get there. Try to be as specific as possible and after the first year (and every subsequent year), review your objectives and ask yourself if they are being achieved. If they are, good, can they be improved? If they are not, consider the reasons why and address those issues. Do not be afraid to modify plans to ensure the success of your business. Recognising the need for adjustment to meet market trends, demands and economic climates is crucial to the success of any business.

Experience, Skills and Training

Your business will only be as good as the skills you possess, so list your relevant skills and the experience gained in these areas. Setting high standards is paramount to any business and reputation. Continuous professional development involves improvement of weak areas and further development of strong areas throughout the lifetime of a business, so be pragmatic when making a list of strengths and weaknesses (see Chapter 1). Doing this highlights the opportunities

for improvement and identifies any training that you will need. Increased levels of skill and professionalism will offer your business greater powers of productivity and market leadership. It is vitally important that cake decoration and design skills match customer expectations, reflect market trends and do not become 'stale' or dated. Ancillary/administrative skills are just as important for a business to be run efficiently: accounting, marketing, selling, telephone techniques, technology, I.T. skills and more. Training is well rewarded. As a new small business you may qualify for government-sponsored training/guidance.

Make a note of the areas in which you feel you would benefit from training. Enquire at your local job centre, contact Business Link or check your local adult education centre for availability.

Any other training fees which may be incurred are usually accepted as a business expense and may be offset against any tax you pay.

Food Hygiene or Food Safety training is required if you are involved in the food trade, however small your food business is when you start. When you register your business with the local authority, the Environmental Health officer will expect you to demonstrate full awareness of food hygiene issues. Courses are run by most local councils, some colleges and private firms; online courses are also available. At present a certificate in Food Hygiene lasts for three years and needs to be updated thereafter (see Chapter 3: Formalities and Procedures).

Benefits of training

- Increases skills and earning potential
- Increases your professionalism
- Increases marketing ability
- Increases confidence
- Alerts you to changes in regulations and/or legislation
- Offers an awareness of currents trends and designs
- Encourages more efficient use of time and skills
- Provides contact with other professionals
- Provides networking opportunities

Formalities and Compliance

All businesses must comply with the relevant regulations and legislation and some of these need compliance before you are able to start trading.

List everything that applies to your business and review annually or as appropriate. Diarise any formalities that require periodic renewal to be certain all applicable legislation is fully complied with at all times (see Chapter 3: Formalities and Procedures).

Markets

Who are your customers, where are your customers, and how will you reach your customers? In order for your business to be successful, you need to identify and continually attract new and potential customers whilst nurturing existing ones. In order to do this you need to have a clear idea of your target market.

If you have previously made cakes from home on a non-commercial basis you may already have an idea of the extent of interest this has generated and the source. This needs to be developed and new markets identified, so how can you plan to do this?

Identify your target customers

Who is going to buy your product? What kind of customers do you want to attract? Your target customers can be identified as people with needs or wants that can be met with the products or services you are able to offer. Your product range will influence the scope of target customers.

Identify your target area

Where are your geographic boundaries that define the area you are able to serve?

Your target market may very well modify as your business develops and/or expands. Be open to opportunities and adapt to meet the needs of changing market demand. This will help to attract new customers and to sell more to existing customers.

Competition and Competitor Analysis

It is a great advantage to know who, where and what your competition is. Research as thoroughly as possible their products and services, who they sell to, what they sell and how much they charge. Once you have this information you can assess the extent of the competition, their apparent strengths and weaknesses, consider how their business may impact on your business ideas and decide whether you can offer something they cannot.

Marketing and Advertising

Creating a marketing strategy is fundamental to any business to tempt and interest potential customers, to show that your product matches their needs, and to let customers know where, who and what you are. For further details refer to Chapter 8: Marketing and Advertising your Business.

Consider your target area limit (a particularly important detail for inclusion on your website) and how you will make contact with customers. Set a budget and then plan what advertising materials your marketing strategy will need to make that contact.

Business Costs

Business start-up costs will differ from business to business but no matter how small or large your intentions may be it is essential to determine the probable extent of financial outlay. Access the Business Link website (see Useful Contacts, page 106) to search its directory of government grants and support services that you may be eligible for: it includes potential sources of assistance with starting up a business, offering information on schemes from central and local government as well as private organisations. Some offer financial assistance (grants), while others offer free or subsidised services such as training or advice.

Initially you will need to calculate how much the set up will cost. Include items that are essential to your day-to-day work, such as:

Food mixer

Baking tins, muffin tins

Baking tools/equipment

Decorating tools/equipment

Protective clothing/workwear

Janitorial supplies such as paper towels, cleaning products

Stationery such as business cards, letterheads, compliment slips, a receipt book

Computer consumables such as printer cartridges, paper

You will also need to include potential initial costs, such as:

Work area refurbishment

Additional telephone line/calls

Business, car and house insurance

Marketing and advertising materials and costs

Computer equipment, peripherals and software

Training

Professional fees, e.g. webpage set up, solicitors

Finally, consider whether there is anything that you don't need now but may do in your first few months of trading and include this in your start-up costs.

Some costs will be one-off whilst others may be periodic so it is important to be fully aware of all the costs which you may incur to allow you to be realistic with budgets and costings. Plan what your business will need, then keep and record all details and receipts as these will be needed to complete your accounts and support any grant application that is made. Further details are given in Chapter 4, pages 46 to 61.

Product Costings

Accurate costing of your product is imperative to allow you to plan and price for profit. Research and complete all costings of products (see pages 48 to 50) and prepare structured price lists (see Pricing for Profit, pages 52 to 55). Whilst it is fundamentally essential to be aware of your competitors' prices, using theirs as a foundation for your own business is inadvisable as each business will differ in their products and services.

Sales

Estimating your annual sales for the first year may not seem straightforward, but there are two important pieces of information that will help: the hours that you are intending to work annually and the income you want to generate. Your estimated sales need to reflect the amount you realistically want to generate. Having created your marketing strategy you will know where your customers are and the likelihood of obtaining orders based on your research.

The first year of trading often shows a variation in estimated sales and this is understandable whilst your business is developing. Your sales figures need to be constantly reviewed: they may reflect a higher than estimated sales figure which is good; on the other hand, if you have lower than expected sales then you will need to ask yourself why. The level and type of sales made is an important indicator of market trends and business success so take notice and modify your business plan to meet diversity, change and customer expectation.

If you find your sales have peaks and troughs unintentionally, consider how you can effect a balance. For example, cupcakes for all occasions offer year-round trade which is of huge benefit to the small business based at home, whilst wedding cakes tend to be seasonal. You can sell cupcakes for baby showers, office parties, Halloween, New Year's Eve, race days, corporate events and sporting events; to say thank you, well done or I'm sorry; to celebrate a new home or exam success; or simply as dinner party take-home gifts: the list is endless and the more versatile you can be, the more potential you will have for year-round sales.

Finance

Plan how you intend to finance your business in the early stages and how you plan to meet not only your business costs but your own personal financial needs. This is vital for any business to succeed. If you need to raise funds, consider contacting your bank or Business Link for advice. A funding offer from family or friends may seem attractive, but you should consider potential consequences very seriously.

Use the sample chart on page 28 to project your cashflow for the first year and record the actual figures so that you can monitor any differences.

On Completion

It may seem a tedious task but taking the time to research and prepare your business plan diligently will be well rewarded. Refer to it regularly to analyse progress, evaluate trends, highlight opportunities and monitor market demands. It will be the cornerstone of your business, bringing together all the information you need to map and build your business. Only with the right knowledge and the right ideas will you give your business the best chance of success.

Business Plan

Business Details

Name of Business		
Business Address		Telephone
		Mobile
		Email
Postcode		Website

Legal Status

Description of Business Products and Services

Business Objectives

Short term

0-12 months

Medium term

1-2 years

Long term

2-3+ years

Experience/Skills

Previous/current

Relevant training

Strengths	Weaknesses

Continued Professional Development Training

Professional Development Training Plan

Formalities and Compliance

☐ Planning and local council	☐ Bank
☐ Mortgagors	☐ Accounts
☐ Environmental Health	☐ Suppliers
☐ Inland Revenue/NI	☐ Professional advice
☐ Insurance	☐ Other (details)
☐ Trading Standards	

Additional Information

Markets and Competition

Target Market Details

Potential Customers and Demography

Market Demand Evidence

Seasonal

Competition - Name	Details/comparison/analysis

Impact/Effect on Own Business

Marketing Stategy	☐ Local	☐ National	☐ E-commerce

Details

Advertising Plan/Materials

£

Business Costs, Sales and Finance

Start-up Costs	£		£

Start-up Costs Funding Source

Product Costing Completed?

£

Anticipated Sales: Year 1

Estimated Annual Running Costs: Year 1

Own Financial Contribution to Business

Personal Financial Needs

Projected Cashflow Business Name Year End

Month	January		February		March		April		May		June		July		August		September		October		November		December	
	Forecast	Actual	Forecast	Actual	Forecast	Actual	Forecast	Actual	Forecast	Actual	Forecast	Actual	Forecast	Actual	Forecast	Actual	Forecast	Actual	Forecast	Actual	Forecast	Actual	Forecast	Actual
Income																								
Sales																								
Other																								
Other																								
A: Total Income																								
Expenditure																								
Ingredients																								
Materials																								
Equipment																								
P & PL Insurance																								
Other Insurance																								
Car Insurance																								
Car Expenditures																								
Telephone																								
Advertising																								
Stationery																								
Postage																								
Computer Items																								
Janitorial																								
Fuel																								
Personal Drawings																								
NI																								
Other																								
B: Total Expenditure																								
Net Profit (A-B)																								

- Planning Consent

- Mortgagors

- Environmental Health

- Business Name

- Tax and National Insurance

- Trading Standards

- Insurance

- Accounting System

- Bank Accounts

- Solicitors

- Copyright, Trademarks and Logos

- Data Protection

Formalities and Procedures

With the initial business plan finalised, next on the agenda are the formalities and procedures that need to be in place before you start trading. Some of these formalities must be completed in order to comply with all compulsory legislation and regulations and others to fulfil obligations laid down by relevant authorities.

There are a number of areas in which you will need to meet the required obligations before you will be permitted to start trading. These are:

- Planning consent

- Mortgagors

- Environmental health

Without approval in these three areas, you will be unable to start your cake decorating business from home.

Other important areas which you will require your attention are:

- Business name

- Tax and National Insurance

- Trading Standards

- Insurance

- Accounting system

- Bank accounts

- Solicitors

- Copyright, trademarks and logos

- Data protection

Planning Consent

It is unlikely you would need planning permission to work from home provided there is no major change of use, for example, you are not employing staff, there is not a significant increase in traffic or people calling and it does not involve activities unusual in

a residential area. It is, however, essential that you check with your local planning authority to confirm that your business will not breach regulations.

If you were to convert part of your home exclusively for business use, such as a garage into a workshop or an outbuilding into a commercial kitchen, you may be liable for business rates.

Contact your local planning authority, advise them in full of your proposed intentions and seek documented consent and approval. Keep and file all documentation. Remember that their approval is based on the information you give them, so you will need to contact them and seek their advice should your situation change.

You will also need to check the deeds/title to your property and any tenancy agreement to ensure you are not restricted or prohibited from running a business from home. This applies to all dwellings including mortgaged and rented property, listed buildings, flats, maisonettes, floating water homes, barges or any armed forces accommodation. If you own a freehold property outright, there may be a deed of covenant with restrictions of use for your property. If you are in any doubt consult a solicitor.

Mortgagors

You will be required to notify your mortgagor, or anyone who holds a financial interest in your property, of your intention to run a business from home.

Seek documented consent and approval, and file securely.

Environmental Health

From 1 January 2006, EU (European Union) food hygiene legislation has applied throughout the European Community. Anyone who owns, manages or runs a food business is affected by the Food Hygiene Regulations 2006 (there are specific regulations in England, Scotland, Wales and Northern Ireland). This includes all home cake makers, whether you sell for profit, fundraising, or make for charity. The regulations do not apply to food cooked at home for private consumption.

The Environmental Health Department executes and enforces these regulations and you must comply with them before you start trading. You will also need to register your business with your Environmental Health Service at least 28 days before you start trading.

Registration is free and most authorities will keep you updated with any new developments on hygiene issues.

Once registered with the Environmental Health Service your premises will be subject to periodic inspections. The frequency will be determined by the initial visit.

Food hygiene regulations

The Food Hygiene Regulations 2006 set out the hygiene requirements for your business. You can view or download copies from the Office of Public Sector Information website: **www.legislation.gov.uk**. The regulations do not apply to food cooked at home for private consumption.

The regulations require all food businesses to put into place a 'food safety management system' to show what you do to make food safely and have this written down. The regulations are flexible, so the procedures can be in proportion to the size of your business, the type of work you do and the ingredients you use. This means that many small businesses using low-risk products will be able to implement very simple but safe procedures and maintain undemanding records. Fresh cream, however, is considered a high-risk product and safety procedures are more stringent.

To help you comply with the regulations, the Food Standards Agency (FSA) has produced a 'Safer Food Better Business' (SFBB) for Caterers' guidance pack in English, Welsh and Chinese. There is also a DVD guide available in 16 different languages. You can view it online at **www.sfbbtraining.co.uk** and/or download it to your computer. The pack contains forms which are designed to be used for the records and documentation that you will maintain. You can use these forms or use forms from other sources (although the ones contained in the FSA pack are particularly useful and give clear information on what is needed). This pack and the Hygiene Regulations 2006 can be downloaded or viewed from their website. The pack (which extends to over 90 pages) has been produced by the FSA in England, Scotland, Wales and Northern Ireland. It is clearly written, informative and an invaluable source of help and advice for caterers. It covers such areas as cross contamination, cleaning, chilling and cooking and includes diaries, record sheets and schedules in template form. Any queries can be answered via your local Environmental Health Officer who enforces the regulations, or by contacting the Food Standards Agency directly.

Two further excellent publications from the FSA are 'Starting up - Your first steps to running a catering business' and 'Food Hygiene – A Guide for Businesses'. Both guides are available to download from the FSA website, or if you would like to order a copy of either of these packs or the DVD call 0845 606 0667 or email foodstandards@ecgroup.co.uk.

For copies of the Welsh versions of SFBB, please contact Andrew Morris in FSA Wales on 029 206 78960 or email him at Andrew.Morris@foodstandards.gsi.gov.uk.

Food hygiene training

The Food Hygiene Regulations require all food businesses to put into place food safety management systems and this includes training. In some cases training is not compulsory, although you are required to demonstrate a thorough knowledge and understanding of food hygiene. Your local Environmental Health Officer will advise on any training required and this will also be partly influenced if you use any high-risk ingredients such as fresh cream.

Training is highly recommended and greatly beneficial to any caterer. Certificated courses are run on a regular basis and range from basic to advanced levels. Topics covered on these courses include cross contamination, temperature control and requirements, bad bacteria, correct storage and safe food handling to name but a few. The entry-level courses take only a few hours to complete and can be accessed and completed online. The more advanced courses, which personally I would recommend, cover a greater depth of knowledge and are particularly interesting and beneficial. It is a worthwhile investment in your business and being aware of possible risks and contamination is crucial.

Contact your local Environmental Health Officer, search online or contact your local adult education centre for further information on these courses.

Complying with the regulations

Complying with the relevant regulations is more often than not very straightforward and a matter of common sense, awareness and high standards of hygienic working practices. Your Environmental Health Officer will expect you to demonstrate a full knowledge of safe working practices and preferably hold a current certificate in Food Hygiene. They will ask you for this information. You are required by law to comply, and demonstrate that you are able to:

- Make sure the food you supply is prepared in a hygienic environment and is safe to eat.

- Identify any food hazards and take steps to eliminate the risks.

- Ensure safe and hygienic procedures are in place, regularly maintained and reviewed.

The regulations focus on hygiene principles and how to identify food safety risks in general terms, and on your own premises. The regulations also acknowledge that some of the guidelines would not be practical in premises used primarily as a private dwelling, and therefore there are variations in the requirements without compromising safety or hygiene. Wherever food is prepared and/or sold you are required to be certain of two main points:

- Your premises are suitable for the purpose of your business and you have adequate and hygienic facilities for the preparation of food at every stage.

- Your working procedures do not expose food to the risk of contamination.

Hygienic facilities

Premises differ greatly, especially domestic kitchens. However, the following key points are of particular importance for any business. You must ensure that your work areas:

- Are thoroughly clean and in good repair.

- Have surfaces which are easy to clean and sanitise (including walls, floors and worktops).

- Are maintained with a regular cleaning schedule.

- Provide adequate facilities to wash and prepare food and equipment.

- Provide a good supply of clean drinking water with proper drainage (normally the kitchen sink). Water is generally supplied through a mains water system and if you are on a private water supply, contact your environmental department for guidance.

- Have sufficient lighting and ventilation.

- Have sufficient, suitable and hygienic storage facilities, including cupboards and fridges.

- Offer separate hand-washing facilities with materials for cleaning hands and drying them hygienically.

- Have hygienic and safe waste disposal, i.e. clean bins with lids.

You must also ensure that you:

- Put forward and implement measures to protect against pests, e.g. mice, fleas and mites.

- Provide toilet facilities which do not lead directly into food preparation areas.

Personal hygiene

You, and anyone who helps you, are required to maintain high standards of personal hygiene. In particular:

- Wash your hands regularly and thoroughly with antibacterial soap/liquid before and during the process of handling food. Dry on disposable hand towels.

- Always wash your hands after visiting the toilet, touching pets (which must not be present during any food preparation processes), handling raw food (including eggs), and disposing of or handling waste/rubbish.

- Wear clean, protective clothing such as white overalls, and wear protective, food-grade gloves.

- Do not smoke in any food preparation areas.

- Hair must be tied back and preferably covered to prevent hair entering and contaminating food or becoming entangled in machinery.

- Jewellery, nail varnish, removable nail art, false nails, acrylic nails and false eyelashes should not be worn as these can become dislodged, fall into and contaminate food. Where cultural beliefs dictate that jewellery must be worn, be certain there is no risk or compromise to food safety/hygiene.

- You should not prepare/work with food if you are ill, particularly if you are suffering from diarrhoea or vomiting or if you have an infected wound, boils, etc.

- Always cover small cuts with blue plasters which can be seen easily should they fall off.

- Never lick utensils or pick at food as saliva contains millions of bacteria.

- If you touch your face, hair, nose or mouth you must wash your hands before proceeding with any food preparation.

Pets

Animals must not be allowed in any areas where food preparation for business purposes is undertaken. There are no exceptions to this. It is essential that pets and their food dishes are kept away from any food preparation area and under no circumstances should they be allowed on the work surfaces. Animal hair gets everywhere, and harbours bad bacteria and germs (as does human hair). It is vital that you wash your hands after touching animals.

How to reduce risk

By simply looking at your work areas to see if there is anything that may jeopardise you or the safe and hygienic production of your cakes, you can take steps to reduce risks. For example:

Risk	Solution
Do you have everyday clutter on your worktops which could find its way into any food being prepared? Small items such as pen tops, pins, buttons, staples, children's toys, paper clips, postage stamps, food ties, etc., can easily find their way into food. Plants and flowers attract insects.	Operate a clear worktop policy: clear everything off worktops including plants, flowers, pens, paper, CDs and books. Work with the minimum of tools and equipment required and always put away after use.
Are your electrical sockets and your equipment safe?	Check sockets and equipment for frayed wires, loose connections and insecure fittings. If in doubt consult a qualified electrician. Diarise for regular checks.
Do you have difficulty reaching high cupboards, shelves or units?	You are responsible for your own safety. Use a proper stepladder and put it away after use.
Are knives properly stored?	Ensure all knives are stored securely and safely, not thrown haphazardly into drawers. Consider using knife blocks or magnetic wall strips.
Is your fridge running at the correct temperature? Is it overloaded? An overloaded fridge is inefficient and poses a risk as the food has little chance of remaining at the correct, safe temperature.	Check the temperature of your fridge and use a fridge thermometer if one is not factory installed. Organise and plan the ingredients you buy so that you don't have too much in the fridge at once.

Risk	Solution
Are the ingredients in your fridge correctly stored?	Keep raw foods at the bottom and fresh foods at the top. Keep meat and fish in sealed containers at the bottom of the fridge.
Are your records up to date?	Organise a routine to ensure your hygiene practices are regularly checked. Refer to SFBB (see page 33).
Are all cake ingredients stored safely?	There must be no risk of cross contamination to cake ingredients where they are not stored independently in fridges, cupboards or drawers. Rearrange storage of ingredients if necessary to ensure you are storing food safely.

The three most common areas of risk for home cake makers are:

! Cross contamination.

! Storage problems.

! Foreign objects in food.

Cross contamination is the transfer of harmful bacteria to food or utensils. Contamination can occur when one food touches another (e.g. raw meat dripping onto cooked or ready-to-eat foods) or when contaminated tools and equipment, surfaces or hands come into contact with food. Cross contamination is a serious source of potential food poisoning (along with not cooking food properly). The main causes of cross contamination can be easily avoided by taking a few simple steps:

1   Wash your hands before undertaking any food preparation.

2   Always wash your hands thoroughly after touching raw food such as meat, eggs (see note overleaf, raw vegetables or fruit, after handling rubbish/waste, and after visiting the toilet.

3   Use disposable, food-grade, protective gloves when handling food.

4   Ensure worktops are scrupulously clean by sanitising regularly with an appropriate antibacterial or steriliser fluid. Refer to SFBB for recommended products (see page 33).

5   Use disposable dishcloths and change regularly.

6   Use disposable hand towels in preference, or reusable hand towels which are changed regularly and used only for this purpose.

7   Never store cooked and raw foods together, either whilst shopping or in the kitchen. Store uncooked meats in sealed containers at the bottom of the fridge. Keep unwashed fruit and vegetables away from cooked or ready-to-eat food and ingredients.

8   Always use separate cutting boards for raw and cooked foods.

9   Always have a separate work board for cake decoration use only.

10 Never lick utensils or pick at food.

11 Insects carry millions of bacteria and can contaminate food as soon as they land on it. Keep food properly covered. Keep flies and all other insects away from food preparation areas by wiping up spills immediately (especially sugar as it attracts insects), emptying rubbish/waste bins regularly (wash your hands immediately afterwards) and keeping the lid on rubbish/waste bins.

12 Store all cleaning fluids/products/chemicals away from any food preparation areas.

13 Take care when using fresh flowers, berries or leaves on cakes, cupcakes or cookies. Many are harmful if ingested and should not come into contact with food, or form part of a decoration.

14 Always ensure any decoration used is of food-grade quality (i.e. approved for food contact) if it is to come into contact with the cake. The food is then adequately protected against chemicals that might transfer onto/into food from non-food-grade materials, possibly causing harm or affecting the quality of the cake. Consider using food-grade separators such as clear acrylic separator discs or cake boards where items that are non-toxic but not food-grade are used.

The Food Standards Agency recommends using only pasteurised egg in any food that will not be cooked (or only lightly cooked).

If you decide to use fresh egg white always use eggs bearing the Lion mark, which guarantees that they have been produced to the highest standards of food safety. All Lion Quality eggs come from British hens vaccinated against salmonella, are fully traceable and have a 'best before' date on the shell as a guarantee of freshness. This is particularly important for cake makers and decorators as you may well use eggs for baking and preparing icings, marzipans and cake fillings.

Eggs can carry bacteria, so always wash your hands before and after handling eggs. Cracked or dirty eggs should not be used. Good hygiene should always be practised when preparing any food. For more information and advice, contact the Food Standards Agency or the British Egg Information Service.

These are just a few examples of how to avoid cross contamination. Further reading and information can be obtained from your local Environmental Health Officer, reputable websites and libraries.

Storage guidelines should be followed to avoid health and safety risks. Sufficient space is needed for ingredients, supplies and cakes. Once cooked, most cakes should be stored in a clean, cool, dry place. Of particular concern to the Environmental Health Officer would be the use of any high-risk products such as fresh cream. You will need to demonstrate that there are adequate storage facilities and maintain appropriate food safety records. This would extend to the storage of any cakes, cupcakes or cookies filled or covered with fresh cream. Good storage practices for food production would include, for example:

- Storage of dry ingredients according to manufacturer's instructions, checking sell-by dates and rotating stock.

- Allocation of a separate cupboard or area for business use.

- Opened packages resealed to avoid the risk of cross contamination and infestation.

- Storage off the floor (the internal base shelf of most kitchen units is elevated from floor level by approximately 10cm).

- Additional refrigeration space as appropriate to meet the needs of the business.

Foreign objects in food are a risk that can be avoided by operating a clear worktop policy and addressing personal hygiene risk areas. Whilst working, use only the tools and equipment required.

I would never recommend using pins in any part of cake production. Use a scriber for marking designs onto a cake; to attach ribbon to a cake board, secure the ends with softened sugarpaste or similar.

Avoiding the use of inedible decorations altogether may not always be possible: ribbon, flower picks and cake top figures are often used. Remember to advise the customer and seek their acknowledgement accordingly (see Important Information Forms on page 65).

When using small decorations which, though edible, may pose a choking risk (e.g. sugar diamonds, candy pearls or dragées), remember to advise the client.

Transport

The regulations stipulate that vehicles used to transport foods must be kept clean and maintained in good condition to protect foods from spoilage/contamination. If you use your vehicle to transport other things in addition to the cakes, then they need to be separated with no risk of cross contamination. Taking the dog or cat in the car at the same time as delivering a cake simply would not be acceptable, neither would muddy football shoes, wellingtons or petrol cans left in the boot! For safety and hygiene after thorough cleaning and/or disinfecting, consider using either large cover sheets or transportation boxes kept only for that purpose. You will also need to ensure cakes are kept at the appropriate temperatures to avoid spoilage; this in particular relates to fillings/coverings such as buttercream, ganache, chocolate and cream. The delivery distance and time involved would determine what you would need to do to maintain safe transport temperatures: freezer blocks, cool boxes or air conditioning, for example.

Home safety

When using your home partly as a business it is a good idea to review basic safety equipment regularly.

- Make sure you have a first aid box and check the contents are in date. Sterile blue plasters are used in the catering business as they are easily detectable and highly visual should they fall off. These are readily available from high street chemists.

- Make sure you have a fire blanket/extinguisher that is in date. Check that all smoke alarms and fire alarms are working and tested regularly. Fire safety information, available in many languages, can be viewed at **www.fireservice.co.uk/safety/hfra.php** and home assessments can be arranged. For the Deaf or hard of hearing visit **www.avonfire.gov.uk** where information can be viewed in British Sign Language.

- Store all cleaning products/chemicals securely and out of the reach of children or vulnerable adults. They should not be stored in a food preparation area.

Food labelling

Selling cakes as a business requires you to label your products with certain information to comply with the Food Labelling Regulations 1996. The regulations can be viewed and downloaded at **www.opsi.gov.uk** or paper copies are available from The Stationery Office (see Useful Contacts, page 107). Since 1st September 2010, the responsibility for food labelling legislation and policy has been split across three government departments: the Department for Environment Food and Rural Affairs (Defra), the Food Standards Agency (FSA) and the Department of Health.

- Defra is responsible for labelling legislation in England that is principally non-safety and for the coordination of labelling policy across Government.

- The FSA is responsible for legislation on labelling and standards that are principally safety based.

- The Department of Health is responsible for nutrition labelling policy in England.

The extent of information required to be declared depends on the type of product being sold and how. Foods which are prepacked by you for direct sale to the customer from either your home, stall or vehicle are exempt from many of the regulations (exemption details can be located in regulations 23 and 27). At the time of writing you are only required to declare:

- The name of the food (regulation 23).

- Whether any additives are present, in which case you must list the category of any of these additives: Antioxidants, Sweeteners, Colours, Flavour Enhancers, Flavourings and Preservatives (regulation 24), e.g. "Contains Colour and Preservative".

- Whether it contains GM (genetically modified) or irradiated foods (regulation 25).

The above information must be clear and unambiguous, with a plain typeface, indelible and not in any way hidden, obscured or interrupted. It must be:

- On the packaging, or

- On a label attached to the packaging, or

- On a label clearly visible through the packaging, or

- On a notice displayed in a prominent position near the point of sale.

However, if your cakes are prepacked (unless in transparent crimp case packaging) and sold onto third parties, such as catering establishments or retail shops, then you are not exempt and will be required to provide General Food Labelling Requirements (regulation 5), which will include the name of the food, durability dates, ingredients (including all additives), place of origin, quantities of certain ingredients, business name and address, storage conditions, and cooking instructions (if relevant). It must be stressed that this is a very general list of labelling requirements for food sold to third parties. Some food products are partially or fully exempt, and others are subject to further legislation specifically relating to them (such as honey, jam and chocolate).

Trading Standards enforce the labelling regulations and are happy to comment on new labels in their draft stage. It is important to contact your local office to be certain you are in compliance. Visit **www.tradingstandards.gov.uk**.

Allergens

The rules for labelling allergens do not apply to foods sold loose or foods sold prepacked for direct sale: **see www.food.gov.uk/foodindustry/ guidancenotes/labelregsguidance/ foodlabelregsguid** for food labelling regulations guidance notes and **www.food.gov.uk/multimedia/ pdfs/publication/allergenlabelguidance09.pdf** for guidance on allergen labelling. However, the Food Standards Agency has provided guidance on the voluntary provision of allergen information on food sold loose or prepacked for direct sale. See **www.food.gov.uk/safereating/allergyintol/label/**. Allergens in food can cause an allergic reaction in some people which may lead to serious illness or even a life threatening situation. Allergens may be present in the ingredients you use or they may be in the food as a result of cross contamination. Currently, The Food Labelling (Declaration of Allergens) (England), (Wales) and (Scotland) Regulations 2009 state the allergens to be listed are:

- Cereals
- Crustaceans
- Eggs
- Fish
- Peanuts
- Soybeans
- Milk
- Nuts
- Celery
- Mustard
- Sesame seeds
- Molluscs
- Lupin (often as seeds/flour and related to peanuts)
- Sulphur dioxide and sulphites (preservatives sometimes used in food and drink)

Cakes containing fresh cream as a covering, filling or topping need to be stored at temperatures below 8°C to maintain their safety. At the time of writing a durability date is not compulsory for cakes sold from home for direct sale.

Because of the natural variance in food, the labelling regulations are comprehensive, extensive and subject to change. The notes above are provided for guidance only as businesses will differ depending on the types of cakes produced and how these are sold. It is important that you comply with the regulations for the purposes of your own business. Contact Defra, who are responsible for the regulations, and your local Trading Standards, who enforce the regulations, to discuss your situation and they will clarify your obligations for the purpose of your business (see Useful Contacts, pages 106 to 107).

Obtaining approval for your premises

You need to register your business with the Health Authority at least 28 days before you start trading. Once you have read through the literature and considered the obligations and requirements needed for your business, reassess your own kitchen and work spaces and address any areas that need attention.

Make a note of any queries you may have or points that need clarifying and speak again with the Environmental Health Officer. Their help and advice is invaluable and they are only too willing to impart this and help you: the key is to demonstrate and maintain high standards of hygiene and to make you aware of and control risk.

Once you register your business with your local Environmental Health Service an initial visit to your property will be made. The officer will undertake an inspection of your kitchen/work areas and have a chat with you about hygiene, cleaning schedules, the type of ingredients you will be using and how you will store them, and any training that you have or need. When she/he is satisfied that everything is in order, and this may mean more than one visit, you will receive approval and you will be able to start production. Future periodic inspections may be made, the frequency depending on the nature and scale of the business.

The Food Hygiene Regulations 2006 are subject to periodic amendments and once your business is registered with the Environmental Health Service, they will normally keep you advised of any issues relevant to your business.

Keep and file any documentation.

Business Name

Chose and finalise a name for your business. If using a website, try to obtain the same domain name (see Choosing and using a Business Name on page 19).

Tax and National Insurance

If you start working for yourself you must register with the Inland Revenue as self-employed within three months of starting your business. You need to register even if you are not paying tax. The Inland Revenue provides a wide range of helpful, clear and informative booklets and a dedicated telephone number specifically for those starting up a new business. The Inland Revenue's Business Education and Support Team offers free courses on a variety of subjects throughout the country, especially for new businesses. You will learn about specific tax and National Insurance issues, be able to discuss your own situation, and be given reference materials for home use. Their workshop for the newly self-employed covers how to register your business with HMRC, the NI contributions you will need to make and whether you are able to qualify for exemption, basic record keeping, allowable expenses, motoring expenses, claiming for equipment and more. It is worthwhile contacting them before you start trading so queries may be resolved and documentation dealt with, leaving you to focus on running yours business (see Useful Contacts on pages 106 to 107).

Trading Standards

The Trading Standards Institute enforces the laws that govern goods and services bought, hired or sold. It is important that any claim you make about your business can be substantiated and anything that you sell is exactly as described. For example, if you declare that your cakes are filled with buttercream, then it must only be buttercream made with butter and not other butter-like fats such as margarine or shortenings. The same applies if you cover your cakes with a nut covering that doesn't contain almonds: you cannot claim they are covered in almond paste or marzipan; and if you use chocolate flavour cake covering you cannot say that it is chocolate. When creating brochures, websites, leaflets and any other promotional material, be certain that any details you provide are correct, unambiguous and not misleading.

Insurance

Every small business will require some level of insurance and it is no different if you are working from home. The three most important areas when running a cake decorating business from home are:-

- Home insurance
- Car insurance
- Product and public liability insurance

Home insurance

It is important to notify your home insurers of a change in circumstances and your intentions to run a small business from home. You will need to gain their approval in writing. Failure to do so may result in a future claim being refused. There may be an increase in premium if they consider there will be a higher risk, so make sure you include this in your annual running costs (see page 28).

Car insurance

This is a legal requirement if you drive and you will need to advise your insurers of your business intentions and the expected extent of activity. They will inform you of any additional premium this may incur. Keep them advised of any future changes no matter how small and be certain you have the appropriate cover for your needs.

Product and public liability insurance

This covers your liability to visitors and members of the public if your business causes illness or injury. Public liability insurance provides cover against claims made by members of the public if they injure themselves whilst on your property and claim you to be responsible, e.g. a customer might slip on a wet floor or trip over a broken step. Product liability insurance protects you against injury claims from your customers through the products you supply, e.g. someone breaks a tooth on a foreign object in the food you supplied or you cause accidental food poisoning. Remember you must take all reasonable care, and demonstrate responsibility and safety precautions, otherwise a claim may be invalidated. Public and product liability insurance is currently only voluntary for most businesses but it would be extremely unwise to operate without it.

A growing business may have additional insurance needs in the future so seek advice from your Business Link advisor and contact your insurers.

Accounting System

Every successful businessperson needs to know their current financial position by maintaining an accurate and up-to-date set of accounts. This information is required by the Inland Revenue, but it also allows you to review your business on a regular basis, track progress, identify problems and take any remedial action. Initially, for a small business, only simple bookkeeping skills are necessary to maintain a set of accounts. Training is offered via the Inland Revenue or you can contact Business Link or your local adult education centre for courses (see Chapter 2, Training on page 22). Keep all receipts, invoices and details of expenses incurred as the Inland Revenue may wish to view these. When using your car for business you will need to provide dated evidence of business mileage. Record the dates, purpose and journey length each time you take a business trip to support your claim.

Set aside time to bring your accounts up to date on a regular basis. Eventually you may wish to consider a software accounting system or use an accountant. Remember to back up all computerised data.

Bank Accounts

No matter how small your business is it is sensible to keep your personal finances separate from those of your business.

Visit your local high street banks and check online to see what each has to offer. Approach your own bank as they already know you: this is useful if you need help in financing your business either now or in the future as they are already aware of your background.

Nearly all high street banks will offer an introductory period of free business banking, often for up to two years subject to terms and conditions. Some also offer interest on your business current account whilst others offer indefinite free business banking operated online, with no branch involvement. Carefully look into any additional costs which may be incurred and costs after any introductory rates expire. Consider your future needs and whether your chosen bank account can grow to meet these needs.

Nearly all the big banks will offer business start-up packs with a copious amount of useful information and fact sheets relevant to financial issues other than banking. Some include software for accounting systems and they can help you to plan and control your finances and offer guidance. Local banks often have local knowledge and this can be quite valuable.

Plan to have your bank accounts fully operational before you start trading.

Solicitors

At some stage you may need the services of a solicitor, whether it is for checking any terms and conditions you want to apply, your business name, your legal position with regard to deposits and payments or to run a professional eye over the wording on your brochures/leaflets. Lawyers For Your Business is a network of 1,000 solicitor firms in England and Wales offering specialist advice to small businesses. Lawyers who participate in this scheme offer a free half-hour initial consultation with a solicitor in your area and advice can be sought on a range of legal issues. They also offer guides for starting a business which can be downloaded from their website **www.lawsociety.org.uk/choosingandusing/ helpyourbusiness/foryourbusiness.law**, ordered by phone or by writing to the Law Society (see Useful contacts on page 106). Taking professional advice can often save you money and protect your business.

Copyright, Trademarks and Logos

Copyright is a set of exclusive rights held by the creator of an original work and gives protection to the creator against the usage of their intellectual property. You are not permitted to use any designs that are protected by copyright without the owner's permission.

Copyright applies to many types of work, such as websites, drawings, designs, photographs, music, books, theatre, software, television and film.

The laws relating to copyright are of particular importance to cake businesses when requested to make cakes featuring TV and film characters, children's cartoon figures, novelty puppets, branded items, trademarks, logos and so on. You may also be asked to copy another cake maker's design for a customer. Doing so without permission from the owner would infringe copyright law so you should only copy or use a work protected by copyright with the owner's permission. If you breach copyright you may be liable to a substantial fine. For full information on Intellectual Property Ownership see **www.ipo.gov.uk** (see also Useful Contacts, page 106).

Using only your own designs enables you to build up a portfolio of your original work and will help to define your own unique style.

Data Protection

The Data Protection Act (DPA) 1998 governs the use of personal information by businesses and other organisations in order to protect the right of individuals to privacy. You will need to comply with the act if you are processing personal information about your customers as part of your business. There are strict, enforceable principles of good practice which you will be bound by, especially those of confidentiality.

These require that personal information is:

- Fairly and lawfully processed.

- Processed for limited purposes.

- Adequate, relevant and not excessive.

- Accurate.

- Not kept longer than necessary.

- Processed in accordance with the date subjects rights.

- Secure.

- Not transferred to countries without adequate protection.

In short, whatever information your customer gives to you must be regarded as confidential, kept securely and not divulged to other parties unless the customer agrees.

The DPA is enforced by the Information Commissioner's Office and full details can be found on their website at **www.ico.gov.uk**. They have produced an excellent series of guidance notes which are clear and straightforward and explain your responsibilities, including 'Getting it right – a brief guide to data protection for small businesses' and a quick 'How to comply' checklist. These guidance notes can be viewed and downloaded from their website, see Useful Contacts on page 106 for further contact details.

The formalities and procedures may seem overwhelming but in reality, it is not an arduous task. You will already be familiar with a considerable amount from your own personal and family needs such as insurance, bank accounts, your mortgage and even privacy – how often have any of us heard, 'Sorry, I cannot give you that information'? So, work through them step by step (some you will only need to do once), file documentation, and when all is complete, you are free to focus on what you really want to do – make cakes!

- Business Costs

- Pricing Structures

- Pricing for Profit

Costs, Pricing and Profit

To survive and be successful in business it is vital that you know exactly what your business costs are. This provides you with the capacity to control, plan, budget and price for profit.

Accurate costing charts are a lifeline to any business – they tell the whole story to date. This allows you to make informed decisions about your business and ascertain whether it is going in the right direction or whether there are changes that need to be made. Sample charts are provided at the end of this chapter for you to use (see pages 56 to 60).

Business Costs

Business costs include all expenditure that is necessary for you to operate the business. These generally fall into three distinct categories:

- **Labour**
- **Cake costs** (i.e. ingredients and materials)
- **Overheads** (i.e. all other costs incurred to allow you to produce and sell cake)

Only when each of these costs is known is it possible to formulate a price list.

Labour

You may already know the time involved in the various stages of production, but if not, start to keep an accurate record. The labour involved should be justifiable, i.e. an efficient and skilled work period. A proportion of the final cake price will be dependent on the labour involved which needs to be justified to enable you to arrive at a competitive market price. If there are any areas in which you feel further training would benefit you, achieve this as soon as possible. More pertinent skills offer greater efficiency, increased marketing opportunities and a better chance of business success.

You will also need to factor in time spent with clients. Allocate an appropriate appointment period for discussing and taking orders and stick to this. Have everything you need to hand and keep the appointment professional, obliging and effective. The same applies to telephone conversations and emails, whether taking orders, ordering supplies, making enquiries or answering queries. Time is not elastic: it needs to be accounted for and reflected in final cake pricings.

Cake costs

In-depth research and computation of costs is necessary throughout the life of a business. It will enable you to price for profit, produce a well-balanced price list, keep control of funding and be aware of any market commodity price changes which may affect your business. Initially this research may be time consuming but it is, without doubt, time well spent! Everything from cake ingredients to paper cases needs to be costed before a price list can be prepared.

There are generally two distinct areas of cost in every cake:

- **The cake base cost**
- **The decoration cost**

Cake base costs consist of the ingredients and materials needed to produce a cake base. They are the easiest of all costs to calculate as the recipes and quantities are a known factor. Many of the basic ingredients, e.g. butter, flour, sugar and eggs, remain relatively cost stable with few dramatic increases. There will always be exceptions to this such as nuts, dried fruits, and chocolate, or anything that relies heavily of the success of a harvest, one reason to be continually aware of price changes in any business.

Creating detailed charts showing the costs of the different cake bases and sizes provides you with an accurate basis for pricing. Using spreadsheet charts, price adjustments can be made easily and allow you to regularly monitor commodity changes which may affect a business in the short or long term. The charts can be as detailed as required and designed for the recipes to be used (see examples on pages 57 to 59).

Decoration costs, such as different types of coverings and fillings, are straightforward to calculate as they are based on cake size (see sample chart on page 60). For other decoration costs keep a record of the amount and expense of the different materials used for decoration, no matter how small, and a pattern will soon emerge. A commercial venture needs to include all options and ready-made decorations may fulfil an important role in business. Cupcakes and mini cakes with individual, handmade decorations which can be prepared easily and time efficiently would no doubt be cost effective. However, with the popularity of cupcakes, the range quality and standard of ready-made decorations has increased and purchasing ready-made decorations may offer a viable alternative. There is a market for ready-made cake decorations, so be open to new ideas and alternatives and consider what will benefit your business and offer clients the greatest choice and value.

Wedding cakes – when setting prices for these and similar cakes, remember that further decorative materials are often used such as additional cake drums, dowels, specialised decorative materials and storage/transport boxes.

Cupcakes – include the cost of muffin cases and cupcake wrappers.

It is important, therefore, to ascertain what kind of decoration you will offer and to research those costs at an early stage, whilst at the same time being aware of offering the customer the best possible choice and service. If your business is to offer set prices for set designs, then virtually all costs are known and there is little variation so you can move on to pricing. If designs and decorations offered are variable, then each of these costs needs to be researched to be certain of accurate pricing lists and you will need to consider your pricing structure (see overleaf).

Overheads

These include all the running costs for your business, for example business insurance, heating, lighting, energy, telephone, computer consumables, fuel, janitorial supplies, stationery, equipment and any necessary protective clothing. (Remember that this book is aimed at running a cake decorating business from home, and therefore, assumes that no business rents or rates will be incurred.)

Overheads are split into two areas:

- **Fixed costs**
- **Variable costs**

Fixed costs – these are the sums which will be incurred irrespective of the amount of business you generate, e.g. business insurance and telephone rental. Therefore, in all cases, the higher the sales level, the more cost effective the business becomes.

Variable costs – these are the amounts which depend entirely on the number of cakes made, e.g. fuel, postage, computer consumables, heating and lighting. Initially some of these costs can be difficult to determine so it is important to spend time considering the likely figures that may be involved according to your anticipated amount of business. Once your business has been running for a short while, a pattern will emerge realising more accurate costing figures. It cannot be stressed enough that time taken to research costs will be rewarded with a far higher degree of business control, offering a greater chance of success.

Energy costs in relation to cake decorating need to be factored into the cake price. Two pieces of information are needed to calculate energy charges: firstly, the rate per hour you are being charged by your utility provider; and secondly, the power rating of your oven/appliance to be used. Utility bills detail the rate you are being charged for each kWh hour of energy. A kilowatt-hour (symbolized kWh) is a unit of energy equivalent to one kilowatt (1 kW) of power expended for one hour of time. On nearly every appliance there is a label that shows the power of the appliance in watts or kW (1000watts equal 1kW). If this is difficult to access, refer to the manufacturer's instruction booklets for the information.

Create your own charts to record costs using the samples provided at the end of this chapter as a guide and monitor on a monthly basis all areas of costs in relation to sales. After the first year of trading, examine your figures in detail: look at the percentage of sales to costs. Are there savings to be made? Can you negotiate better bulk discounts? Are your sales restricted to the certain months of the year and, if so, how can you generate business outside of these months? Are some products more profitable than others?

As an example, if an oven has a power rating of 2.5kW and is run for 1.5 hours, the units used would be 3.75kWh. Multiply this by the rate the utility company is charging per kWh to arrive at the cost per hour of using an oven.

Pricing Structures

Having completed the research on costs, there are a number of ways to structure a price list. The following three methods are the most common:

1 **Set designs at set prices.**

2 **Variable designs at set prices.**

3 **Individually designed and priced.**

Consider each one in relation to your business and how it matches realistically.

1 Set designs at set prices

A predetermined number of set designs at set prices is the easiest of pricing structures and is commonly found in high street and commercial bakers. All the cost factors are known. The set designs allow you to cost the cakes accurately for both ingredients and time, whether they are wedding, celebration, novelty, themed or cupcakes. Variations in size and colour can be offered to the customer, enabling them to select the most suitable cake for their special occasion. A portfolio to illustrate the range available offers an accessible choice for clients.

2 Variable designs at set prices

A set price allows the customer the flexibility to select from a predetermined range of decorative work, style, size, colour and shape that can be mixed and matched to create a more personal design. This offers the customer a wider choice than the option above with more individuality, but still enables you to predict costs and time accurately. Requests for additional or more detailed work can then be quoted for separately. Portfolio illustrations of your design work and decoration would illustrate the range and possibilities of the design and decoration that could be incorporated within the price category. It is important that it is clear to the customer exactly what is included in the stated price: one person's expectation of a 'small' model is another person's idea of a full-scale model complete with all accessories! If there is to be the option of additional extras, then it would be useful if this were to be explained clearly on price lists and in brochures.

The price level for these cakes will include your predetermined allowance for the cost and time of decorative work. The key to setting a variable price list is to be certain of the cost and time element involved for any type of cake offered. The selection of decorative work, together with the costs of materials, whether handmade or not, should all take more or less the same time to complete and incur as closely as possible the same amount of cost.

Cupcakes, mini or individual cakes can be priced in the same way. Remember to include a higher charge for specialised boxes and offer specialised cupcake wrappers and/or matching cake cases as an optional extra.

3 Individually designed and priced

You may decide to provide a bespoke service offering individually designed cakes made to order. The costs are calculated after the design, style, shape decoration and size are decided upon. A brochure could indicate a 'from' price, but costing figures for both materials and ingredients are essential to enable you to quote accurately for each cake order. A portfolio of bespoke cakes, in all cases respecting both customer privacy and data protection, could offer ideas and indicate likely costs. Novelty cakes can be notoriously difficult to price, especially adult ones which are specifically personalised and more often than not each cake is an individual masterpiece! Avoid committing to a price until you know exactly what is involved. For any commissioned work remember the need to comply with copyright laws in the cake design and data protection of your customers' details.

Portfolio work

Businesses are required to comply with copyright laws and data protection and this includes your portfolio work. Use only your own designs or those you have entitlement to use. Bespoke cake images may only be used when a client has given permission for you to do so.

The decision

You may wish to offer a choice of all three options to your customers as this would open up a wider target market. Limiting a business to a single area may be a disadvantage unless you are certain of strong and continuous markets or are able to diversify when needed. Offering unlimited choice may be a disadvantage unless you are certain of being able to cope with the demand. Make your initial choice carefully, consider where your current skills are, who your likely customers are, and how you want your business to progress. Allow for the possibility of changes in market trends and always be open to change and opportunities.

When you have decided on your pricing structure the next step is to price for profit.

Pricing for Profit

A 'pricing for profit' strategy is probably one of the most important factors in determining whether or not a small business will succeed. Offering customers a high quality product with unparalleled standards of service is another, so it is important to ensure that your prices reflect the products and services that you offer.

Deciding what to charge for a cake depends largely on the production costs and the time involved. However, numerous other factors have a bearing on and influence the price you finally charge, such as:

- Your location
- Your skill level
- Your standards
- Your business image
- What is included in the service offered
- What your competitors charge
- What your customers will pay
- Your target market
- The amount of profit you want to make

All these factors need to be considered in conjunction with one another.

The amount you charge must cover all your costs and must also include a figure which is representative of the time expended to produce the cake/s (see page 48). An adjustment is then made for the market value – the price your cakes will sell for on the open market, your target market. Each of the above factors will affect the final price.

Your location

Your location will have an impact on price. The cost of living differs throughout the UK and what some clients in one area will be happy to pay, others will not. It is vital that you research your target area and make comparisons. A product is only worth what your market will pay.

Your skill level

The greater the skill level in your area of business the greater the opportunity for generating revenue. Being able to offer clients choice allows you to reach a wider target market, thus presenting you with greater selling prospects. High skill standards will often command a greater market respect.

Your standards

A high standard of work can command a higher price. Prices that reflect high standards of service, quality and style can be justified without question. Paying a premium for a mediocre product may only justify an unwelcome reputation and a low market value. A reputation for exceptional levels of professionalism, reliability, quality and service always need to remain a high priority.

Your business image

Business image will often mirror your target market, the type of business you want to create and the type of customers you want to attract. Your image needs to show that you are offering a specialised product and an individual service.

What is included in the service offered

Determine what is included in the prices you are setting. Delivery boxes, specialised cupcake wrappers or cake stand hire, for example, may be an added extra. Make these details clear to avoid any misunderstanding and any loss of goodwill. It is often a great incentive to clients if wedding or similar special occasion cakes can be delivered and set up at their chosen venue so consider whether this could be offered as standard within a limited distance or otherwise. Your business needs to attract potential clients and you need to keep them, so make sure that you are meeting their needs.

What your competitors charge

Be conscious of your competitors' prices but base your prices on your own values. You could easily be misguided in using your competitors' prices as a benchmark only to find their business, service, standards and quality are very different to yours. Find out what your competitors offer by perusing their brochures, information leaflets and websites. Is there something you could offer that they don't?

What your customers will pay

Setting prices too low can seriously damage your business and image. Potential customers may associate exceptionally low prices with a 'cheap and cheerful' image. Furthermore, very small profit margins allow you no room for adjustment. Remember, you may be pricing an order for 12 months ahead and some raw material costs can be quite volatile. At the other end of the scale,

setting prices too high may have a detrimental effect on your business: you can price yourself out of the market and end up with few or no orders. Researching your product costs in depth and taking into account your locality and selling area will offer an accurate guide as to the level customers will pay.

Your target market

Researching and knowing your market is a linchpin to any business. Matching customers' needs with your product provides you with a far better chance of achieving a full order book. Do as much research as possible before you take major business decisions. What is in the locality? What is the demographic profile for your target area? (To find this use a search engine and type in Demographics and the area/postcodes for your target market.) Will your product match their needs? If not, are you willing to adjust?

The amount of profit you want to make

Setting prices needs to be done realistically and match market value. Depending on the size of business you intend to run, prices can be calculated very simply on cake costs, overheads and labour, plus a mark-up for profit. There will be a minimum amount that you will need to charge to cover the total cost of making your cakes: this is always the starting point. How much you add on will depend on the above factors.

Calculating a selling price

1 Work out the cost of the cake: this should include all ingredients, decorations, overheads and labour.

2 Decide what percentage profit is appropriate: the cake cost is the remaining proportion of 100%, e.g. 60% profit with remaining 40% being the cake costs. So, a cake costing £25 with a 60% profit margin would sell for £62.50. The profit can be calculated as follows:

Cake costing £25 with 60% profit: (£25 ÷ 40) x 100 = £62.50 selling price

Cake costing £25 with 70% profit: (£25 ÷ 30) x 100 = £83.33 selling price

3 Once you have calculated the profit margin, check whether the selling price is appropriate for your market based on what you know about your market. If it is too high or too low, you will need to adjust the profit margin in order to change the selling price.

Ultimately a good business will endeavour to keep costs down whilst charging the going market rate, thereby maximising profit.

Calculating a selling price

To calculate a percentage profit margin of your annual turnover, first subtract your annual costs from your turnover: this is your profit. Divide this by your turnover and multiply by 100 to give your profit as a percentage,

e.g. cake sales of £480 per week would result in an annual sales turnover of £25,000. Costs of around £8000 would leave a profit of £17,000, which is around 70%.

Turnover – costs = profit, so 25000 – 8000 = 17,000

(Profit ÷ turnover) x 100 = profit as a percentage, so (17,000 ÷ 25000) x 100 = 68%

As I guide, I would recommend aiming for a 60% profit margin. Anything between 50% and 60% is acceptable, if you can achieve anything over this is you are doing well!

Whether you intend to run the business as a part-time or full-time career, costings are equally important. Making a decision on costing is probably one of the hardest of all so there are further tips to help at the end of this chapter.

Take time to research, consider and plan before making your final decision and it will be time well spent.

Discounts

Having delivered course seminars on 'Starting a Cake Decorating Business from Home' for many years, one of the issues raised by virtually every delegate on the course is that of charging friends (and friends of friends!). Many have reported feeling uncomfortable discussing prices with friends and this is where they frequently take the easy option and do not charge at all, only to regret that decision. Those not involved in cake design and decoration are often unaware of the time and costs involved. I am sure many of you also recognise this situation: you get the party invitation one day and the telephone call/email the next asking you to make the cake! Your business is cakes: the business makes a profit, the profit pays the bills. Trapping yourself into either not making a charge at all or offering uncontrolled discount could lead to a poor chance of survival in business. It may challenge friendships and it may also cause friction between customers when different prices are offered. One of the best pieces of advice I received from Business Link was that 'friends do not ask for discounts – they want your business to succeed'. Of course, it is up to you whether you offer a discount or not, but be certain that you do not end up with an order book full of discounted cakes. It would be unwise to set a precedent which you may later regret.

To avoid embarrassment on either side, overcoming this issue is simple: when the enquiry arrives, have a brochure and price list ready. This brings to their attention the level of cost involved and also assists them in making their choice.

Charity cakes

You may have requests to donate a cake for charity. There may be an occasion when you want to support a particular charity but it is unlikely that any of us would be able to respond positively to every approach made. If you do decide to donate a cake, there may be the opportunity for a mention in the local or national press and you may generate interest from potential customers. Arrange to leave business cards/brochures by the side of the cake or with the organiser.

Pricing tips

Time

- Time used effectively (right skills and ability) and efficiently (time managed) will help to produce the greatest annual profits.

- The more cakes you make at a time the more time efficient your business becomes. Time measuring ingredients is the same for a small or large batch of cakes and you may also make savings on the cost of using your oven. Pro rata, a batch of 100 cupcakes will take very little additional time to that of 50.

Cost

- Decorations purchased in bulk and handmade decorations made in bulk will be more economical as long as you know you will use them. Buy in bulk from reputable suppliers. If storage is a problem, consider sharing larger orders with colleagues/associates.

- Negotiate a trade discount from suppliers. The more you order, the greater discount you can negotiate.

- Plan ahead by checking order books regularly and only order supplies when you need them: stockpiling is dead money (balance this against making bulk savings, see above).

- Avoid being dependent upon one supplier.

- Review costs regularly using costing charts (see pages 56 to 60).

- Compare quality with cost: buying cheaper may mean poorer quality and create more work in the long run.

Setting your prices is probably one of the most difficult and one of the most important decisions you will have to make. By researching thoroughly, calculating your costs meticulously, examining timescales involved, and appreciating the market value, you will have a strong knowledge on which to base your pricing decisions.

Monthly Cost Record	Jan	Feb	March	April	May	June	July	Aug	Sept	Oct	Nov	Dec
P&PL Insurance												
Home Insurance												
Other Insurance												
National Insurance												
Car Insurance												
Car Expenses												
Telephone Line												
Telephone Calls												
Advertising												
Stationery												
Postage												
Computer												
Consumables												
Janitorial												
Fuel												
Cake Ingredients												
Cake Materials												
Equipment												
Other												
Other												
Other												
Other												
Total												
Sales												
NET												

Rich Fruit Cake (round)

Recipe and cake costs as at	15cm/6"		18cm/7"		20cm/8"		23cm/9"		25cm/10"		28cm/11"		30cm/12"		33cm/13"		35cm/14"		38cm/15"	
	Amount	Cost	Amount	Cost	Amount	Cost	Amount	Cost	Amount	Cost	Amount	Cost	Amount	Cost	Amount	Cost	Amount	Cost	Amount	Cost
Butter																				
Muscovado sugar																				
Plain flour																				
Eggs																				
Lemons																				
Spices																				
Brandy/spirits																				
Sultanas																				
Currants																				
Raisins																				
Glacé cerries																				
Ground almonds																				
Chopped almonds																				
Silicone paper																				
Greaseproof paper																				
Sundry																				
Sundry																				
Sundry																				
Total Cost																				

Fillings, Icings and Coverings

Recipe and cake costs as at	15cm/6" Amount	Cost	18cm/7" Amount	Cost	20cm/8" Amount	Cost	23cm/9" Amount	Cost	25cm/10" Amount	Cost	28cm/11" Amount	Cost	30cm/12" Amount	Cost	33cm/13" Amount	Cost	35cm/14" Amount	Cost	38cm/15" Amount	Cost
Marzipan																				
Royal Iced Cakes																				
Icing Sugar																				
Dried Albumen																				
Total																				
Sugarpaste Cakes																				
Sugarpaste																				
Apricot Jam																				
Total																				
Buttercreamed Cakes																				
Icing Sugar																				
Butter																				
Jam																				
Flavourings																				
Total																				
Ganache Filling																				
Cream																				
Chocolate																				
Total																				
Cream Cheese Frosting																				
Cream Cheese																				
Icing Sugar																				
Butter																				
Essence/Flavoring																				
Total																				

Cupcakes/Whoopie Pies

Recipe and cake costs as at _____

	Quantity	Flour	£	Butter	£	Oil	£	Sugar	£	Eggs	£	Nuts	£	Other	Specify	£	Total Cost
Victoria Sandwich Mix	10 medium	200g		200g				200g		4				1tsp	Vanilla essence		
Chocolate														2tbsp	Cocoa		
														1-2tbsp	Milk		
Coconut														25g	Dessicated		
														1-2tbsp	Milk		
Red Velvet Cupcakes	8 medium	150g		60g				150g		1				½tsp	Vanilla essence		
														20g	Cocoa		
														¼tsp	Bi carb		
														1½tsp	Cider vinegar		
														120ml	Buttermilk		
															Foodpaste: red		
Hawaiian Cupcakes	10 medium	200g				85ml		225g		2		60g			Hazelnuts		
														¼tsp	Vanilla essence		
														1	Banana, mashed		
														110g	Crushed pieapple		
														1	Orange zest		
Chocolate Temptation	5 medium	115g		115g				115g		3				½tsp	Vanilla essence		
														10g	Cocoa powder		
														60g	Grated chocolate		
Whoopie Pies	8 large/16 single	450g		125g				200g		1				1tsp	Vanilla extract		
														¼tsp	Bi carb		
														¼tsp	Salt		
														250ml	Buttermilk		

Recipe and cake costs as at	Quantity — Topping for CC or filling for WP	Butter £	Cream Cheese £	Icing Sugar £	Choco-late £	Other £	Specify	Total Cost £	Notes
Buttercream: Basic	10 medium CC / 10 Single WP	125g		250g		½tsp	Vanilla essence		Fresh berries cost+
						2tbsp	Milk		
Chocolate						1tbsp	Cocoa powder		
Rose petal						1tbsp	Rose water		No milk
Cream Cheese: Frosting	10 medium CC / 10 large WP	50g	125g	300g		1tbsp	Vanilla extract		
Lemon CC Frosting						1tbsp	Grated lemon rind		Unsalted butter
Rich		60g	300g	340g					Chill well
White Chocolate Icing	10 medium CC / 10 Single WP	100g		225g	100g		Grated white chocolate		
						15ml	Milk		
White Frosting		140g		140g	100g		Melted white chocolate		
Double Choc Frosting	15 medium CC / 15 Single WP	100g	200g	60g	200g		Dark chocolate		Thicken with more icing sugar if necessary
						200g	Cream		
						1tbsp	Vanilla extract		
Ganache	10 medium poured CC/WP / 6 medium piped	225g			225g		Dark, milk, white chocolate		
Orange						1tbsp	Orange liqueur		
Baileys						2tbsp			
Brandy						2tbsp			
Fondant	15 medium CC / 15 Single WP					250g	Sugarpaste		Flavour as required
						2tbsp	Liquid Glucose		
						2tbsp	Sugar		
Glace Icing	10 medium CC / 10 Single WP			400g		1tbsp	Water		Flavour as required

Celebration Cakes					
	15cm	20cm	23cm	25cm	28cm
Round					
Square					
Novelty					

Choose from our mouth-watering, rich and moist chocolate cake, sumptuous vanilla or carrot cake, and toffee fudge or strawberry cake, all filled with a delicious buttercream and covered in sugarpaste. Browse our extensive cake portfolio and select the design and size to suit your own personal celebration. Delicious!

Children's fun cakes – fantastic!					
	15cm	20cm	23cm	25cm	28cm
My mouse!					
Space adventure					
Crazy crocodile					
Fairy garden					
Jungle magic!					

A choice of children's cakes to enchant and thrill! Funky and fun or full of fairy magic, children (and adults!) will love these creations.

Cupcakes – simply irresistible					
Quantity	10	20	30	40	50
Wedding					
Celebration					
Novelty					
Children's					
Ladies that lunch					

Celebrate in style! Weddings, celebrations, baby showers, 'good luck', hen parties, leaving celebrations, birthdays, corporate days, house moves, and more!

Wedding Cakes					
	15cm	20cm	23cm	25cm	28cm
Summer garden					
Parcels					
Top hat and tails					
Snowflake					
Tropical					
Hearts and roses					
Romance					
Funky fun!					
Chocolate tower					
Wicked and delicious!					
I do					

We believe cakes should look as good as they taste. All our cakes are hand-baked and our designs tailored to suit virtually every occasion, helping to make them memorable and fun Out superb range of styles includes contemporary, abstract, classic and novelty choices. Each design comes in a colour choice to co-ordinate and complement your wedding.

Prices are for the complete cake. Simply browse our portfolio, discuss your preferences and select your design and size. During your consultation we will help and advise on cake sizes and portions. Our amazing cakes come boxed, ready for you to take away. Alternatively, as about our delivery and set-up service, available at an additional cost. Mix and match wedding cakes and cupcakes – the choice is yours. Helping to make your special occasion memorable and fun is our aim and as for our cakes – simply irresistible!

 Kathy Moore Cakes

The Bakery House, Beach Road, Sandborough, Lancashire FY8 123
Telephone: +44 (0) 1253 123 456 Website: KathyMooreCakes@Lime.net

Set designs at set prices

Cakes make every occasion special! Kathy's Cake Inguldence specialises in creating cakes that not only look amazing but taste delicious too. All our cakes are baked by hand with traditional ingredients sourced locally wherever possible, from light, delicate sponge cakes perfect for a summer celebration to luxuriously rich, moist chocolate cakes. Each tier can be a different taste sensation: white chocolate and strawberry, vanilla and rose petal, or a decadent dark chocolate and orange liqueur, each one lavishly decorated with dazzling chocolate swirls, curls and cigarillos – simply irresistible with matching cupcakes! Or choose a rich fruit cake bursting with plump raisins and juicy cherries, a sumptuous and mouthwatering toffee and fudge cake, a carrot cake, or a truffle biscuit cake. Our individual cupcakes are just as tasty and tempting with a whole range of flavours and toppings to choose from; for special occasions, each is finished with a choice of superb cupcake wrappers.

Discuss your ideas and preferences, browse through our portfolio and select from the wide choice of decorating ideas, designs, styles and shapes. We will be delighted to create your cake and help make the occasion memorable and fun. Our delivery and set-up service is available locally and further afield by arrangement.

Telephone to make and appointment – we will be happy to help.

Kathy Moore Cakes

The Bakery House, Beach Road, Sandborough, Lancashire FY8 123
Telephone: +44 (0) 1253 123 456 Website: KathyMooreCakes@Lime.net

Kathy Moore Cakes

The Bakery House, Beach Road, Sandborough, Lancashire FY8 123
Telephone: +44 (0) 1253 123 456 Website: KathyMooreCakes@Lime.net

Decorated Wedding Cakes		
Size	Round	Square/other
15cm	£xxx	£xxx
20cm	£xxx	£xxx
25cm	£xxx	£xxx
31cm	£xxx	£xxx
36cm	£xxx	£xxx

Decorated Cup Cakes		
Quantity	Delectable	Indulgence
10	£xxx	£xxx
20	£xxx	£xxx
30	£xxx	£xxx
50	£xxx	£xxx
100	£xxx	£xxx

Choose the style, flavour, topping and decoration from our exquisite range of cupcakes, delightfully finished with a choice of cupcake wrappers.

Contemporary, abstract, classic, traditional or simply stunning themed creations, all our wedding cakes are hand baked and finished with flair to enchant and thrill. Price includes the decoration of your cake, styled and created from our mix-and-match range. Make an appointment to discuss your needs and browse our extensive portfolio – our range indulges you with designs, styles, shapes and sizes for you to mix and match and create an individual look.

Requests for decorative work in addition to the mix-and-match styles can also be included – this may incur further costs so please enquire.

Choose from wickedly rich and moist chocolate cakes, scrumptious individual cupcakes, deliciously light and mouthwatering sponge cakes and more, then decide on the filling. Indulge yourself – we are happy to help!

www.kathyscakeindulgence.co.uk

Varied designs set prices

- Letterheads
- Compliment Slips
- Business Cards
- Envelopes
- Sales Order Forms
- Important Information Forms
- Invoices and Receipts

Business Forms
and Stationery

Business forms and stationery covers all aspects of your printed material, whether its purpose is to communicate, provide a record, present information, or give instructions.

The types of forms/stationery you are likely to require (but not limited to) include:

- Letterhead paper
- Compliment slips
- Business cards
- Envelopes (and labels for envelopes)
- Sales order forms
- Important information forms
- Invoices and receipts

In order to comply with the Companies Act 2006 (see page 19) certain information must be included on business forms and stationery and be printed in clear, legible characters. As a sole trader you must include your name or business name (if you have chosen a different name other than your own, see page 19), and your address on all business letters, orders and receipts. This includes, for instance, invoices, written orders for goods or services to be supplied to the business, business emails and requests for payment. For full details and further information contact Companies House or Business Link (see useful contacts on page 106). Compliance is compulsory.

Letterheads

Your name, address and contact details must be printed on your business letters. Consider creating your own logo to use for your business and be consistent with the fonts you use.

Compliment Slips

Compliment slips are usually a cut-down version of your letterhead and are a useful alternative when a full letter is not required, e.g. attached to brochures, invoices and receipts.

Business Cards

Business cards identify you and your business and are a very important marketing tool. The details you include are at your discretion.

Envelopes

It is useful to have a return address and logo on your envelopes, not least for marketing purposes. You can either print this onto your envelopes or have labels printed (which can also be used on cake boxes).

Sales Order Forms

You must print your name, address and contact details on your order form.

This is a complete record of the cake commission which you are accepting and which your customer is requesting. It forms a contract between you and your customer and therefore it is important that both parties have a clear and accurate understanding of the order.

Advise customers of any terms and conditions which apply to their order and provide them with a copy (see Chapter 6). When the client has read and agreed to the terms and conditions, and has checked the order, record a customer signature at the bottom of the sales order form. By signing the order form they are acknowledging their agreement to the terms and condition set. Provide the customer with a copy for her/his personal records and keep the original, signed order form filed safely.

The order form (see sample on page 67) can also be used to chart the progress of the commission through to completion. Setting up the charts as a spreadsheet provides the facility to use the order sheet for stock control and to extract other useful information.

Remember to ensure that customer details, confidential and sensitive information is kept secure and out of sight (see data protection, page 45).

On collection of the order, record the customer's signature to confirm receipt of the order in good condition. If you are delivering a cake, a simple form could be used to cover delivery and set up (see page 73).

Important Information Forms

I always recommend that essential safety information is given to the customer regarding their cake order when they collect it or take delivery (see sample form on page 72). In the event that the customer is not going to be cutting the cake, provision is made on the form to confirm that they are responsible for passing on safety information to any involved parties. The completed, signed form should be retained by you and a signed copy given to the customer.

Advising the client of issues such as allergens, additives, inedible decorative items, and other items which, although edible may cause harm if ingested (e.g. sharp pieces of pastillage, or choking hazards such as sugar diamonds or dragées) is vital. The information provided on the sample form is an example only: amend it to suit your own requirements.

Invoices and Receipts

It is a requirement to print your name, address and contact details on your invoices and receipts.

Number and cross reference invoices and receipts with sales order forms and retain copies as they are needed for tax purposes. Include the date the invoice was raised, the date by which payment should be made and how, and a brief description of the sales order.

Expanding businesses may benefit from a business software package for sales orders, invoicing, accounting, product ordering, and other financial processes. Many packages are available although few are geared to the very small business. Decide what is most suitable for you; you can seek advice from Business Link (see Useful Contacts on page 106).

Kathy Moore Cakes

The Bakery House, Beach Road, Sandborough, Lancashire FY8 123
Telephone: +44 (0) 1253 123 456 Email: KathyMooreCakes@Lime.net
Website: www.kathymoorecakes.co.uk

Kathy Moore Cakes

with compliments

The Bakery House, Beach Road,
Sandborough, Lancashire FY8 123.
Telephone: +44 (0) 1253 123 456
KathyMooreCakes@Lime.net

www.kathymoorecakes.co.uk

Kathy Moore Cakes

The Bakery House, Beach Road, Sandborough, Lancashire FY8 123
Telephone: +44 (0) 1253 123 456 Email: KathyMooreCakes@Lime.net
Website: www.kathymoorecakes.co.uk

with compliments

Kathy Moore Cakes

www.kathymoorecakes.co.uk
The Bakery House, Beach Road, Sandborough, Lancashire FY8 123
Telephone: +44 (0) 1253 123 456 Email: KathyMooreCakes@Lime.net

Letterhead, compliment slip and business card examples

Kathy Moore Cakes

The Bakery House, Beach Road, Sandborough, Lancashire FY8 123
Telephone: +44 (0) 1253 123 456 Email: KathyMooreCakes@Lime.net
Website: www.kathymoorecakes.co.uk

Customer Order Form

Name	
Address and postcode	

Telephone and email	Home	Work	Mobile	Other	Email

Occasion	Day		Time		Date
Collection *or*	Day		Time		Date
Delivery venue	Day		Time		Date
	Contact name and tel no. at venue				

Special instructions					

Cake style	single	stacked	tiered	mini	cupcakes	whoopie cakes/other
Number of tiers						
Sizes						
Shape						
Flavour/recipe						
Marzipan?						
Filling(s)						
Icing and colour(s)						
Special instructions						
Design brief - full design details overleaf						

Cake price		£
Delivery/set up		£
Other	details	£
Hire charges	details	receipt no.	£
Deposit paid	Date	receipt no.	£
Balance due	Date		£

Customer signature - order placement	Customer signature - order collection
☐ I have read and agree to the terms and conditions provided	☐ I confirm receipt of above cake order in good condition
Date	Date

See overleaf for customer worksheet (full design details)

Customer Worksheet

Name

Order Completion date			
Occasion	Day	Time	Date
Collection *or*	Day	Time	Date
Delivery venue	Day	Time	Date

Cake style	single	stacked	tiered	mini	cupcakes	whoopie cakes/other
Number of tiers						
Sizes						
Shape						

Flavour/recipe	
Marzipan?	
Filling(s)	
Icing and colour(s)	
Special instructions	
Design details	

☐ Ingredients ordered	☐ Materials ordered	☐ Baking dates	Decorations completed ☐
☐ Received/stocked	☐ Received/stocked	☐	Order completed ☐
		☐	Order checked ☐
		☐	Order paid in full ☐
		☐	
		☐	

Kathy Moore Cakes

The Bakery House, Beach Road, Sandborough, Lancashire FY8 123
Telephone: +44 (0) 1253 123 456 Email: KathyMooreCakes@Lime.net
Website: www.kathymoorecakes.co.uk

Invoice:

Invoice to:

Date:

Customer Reference:

Invoice number:

Order Date:

Details:

Order total:

Amount received:

Payment amount due:

Balance outstanding:

Payment amount due by:

Balance outstanding due by:

You can use the same basic template to create a receipt form

Kathy Moore Cakes

The Bakery House, Beach Road, Sandborough, Lancashire FY8 123
Telephone: +44 (0) 1253 123 456 Email: KathyMooreCakes@Lime.net
Website: www.kathymoorecakes.co.uk

Hire Agreement

Invoice to:	Date:
Address:	Agreement Number:
	Receipt Number:

Details:	Period of hire:
Item/s hired:	Start date:
Item/s hired:	End date:

Hire charges:	Hire charge due:
	Equipment deposit:
	Balance due:

Customer signature
I agree to the terms and conditions as stated

Date:

Equipment return:	Date:
Equipment deposit return:	Amount:

Customer signature
I acknowledge receipt of deposit as stated

Date:

Please see overleaf for terms and conditions

See opposite for terms and conditions to go on the back of this form

Kathy Moore Cakes

The Bakery House, Beach Road, Sandborough, Lancashire FY8 123
Telephone: +44 (0) 1253 123 456 Email: KathyMooreCakes@Lime.net
Website: www.kathymoorecakes.co.uk

Equipment Hire Agreement

The Customer agrees to the following terms and conditions of the Company.

Deposit

In addition to hire fees, a deposit is required for all equipment hired.

The deposit will be reimbursed in full to the Hirer, via the same payment method, upon return of hired equipment on the specified date, provided no damage has been incurred.

Equipment

All hired equipment must be returned on the specified day (unless prior alternative arrangements have been agreed) otherwise extra charges may be levied to cover further hire costs. Collection of hired equipment may be arranged subject to availability and may incur additional fees which will be stated at the time of booking.

Any costs to repair damage to/replace hired equipment will be deducted from the deposit paid.

The equipment on hire shall remain the absolute property of the Company at all times.

The Customer is responsible for checking the equipment to be hired upon receipt. By signing the Equipment Hire Agreement, the Customer acknowledges the equipment is undamaged and in good working order.

Throughout the period of hire the Customer shall be responsible for the safe keeping of the equipment and shall be liable to the Company for all loss of or damage to the equipment howsoever caused.

The Customer shall pay to the Company the full cost of replacing any lost equipment within 28 days. During this time the Customer is required to pay any losses incurred by the Company resulting from the loss of the equipment hired.

Cancellation

Hire charges are refundable if cancellation is made more than three months prior to the Agreement date, less any expenses incurred by the Company, which will be specified at the time of booking equipment hire.

Kathy Moore Cakes

The Bakery House, Beach Road, Sandborough, Lancashire FY8 123
Telephone: +44 (0) 1253 123 456 Email: KathyMooreCakes@Lime.net
Website: www.kathymoorecakes.co.uk

Important Information

To:	Date:
	Customer Reference:

Important information regarding your cake order is given below for which acknowledgement is required prior to the release of the order. By signing below you agree to pass this information to any involved parties.

There are items on this cake which are not edible. These must be removed before the cake is cut and/or consumed.

Details:

Please store cake/s in cool, dry, hygienic conditions

Your cake has been prepared in a kitchen where allergens may be present and therefore may contain traces of the following allergens

- ☐ Nuts
- ☐ Peanuts
- ☐ Cereals
- ☐ Sesame seeds
- ☐ Sulpher dioxide
- ☐ Crustaceans
- ☐ Fish
- ☐ Soya beans
- ☐ Celery
- ☐ Mustard
- ☐ Milk
- ☐ Eggs

Customer signature
I confirm receipt of the above information and my responsibility to inform any involved parties

Date:

Kathy Moore Cakes

The Bakery House, Beach Road, Sandborough, Lancashire FY8 123
Telephone: +44 (0) 1253 123 456 Email: KathyMooreCakes@Lime.net
Website: www.kathymoorecakes.co.uk

Delivery/set up

Delivery to:

Date:
Customer Name:
Time:

Delivery of cake	Set up of cake (Delete as appropriate)
Details	

Received in good condition
Signature:

Print name:

Date:

- Price

- Deposits

- Payment arrangements

- Alterations

- Specifications of the Order

- Collection, Delivery and Set-up

- Cancellation and Refunds

- Copyright

- Publication and Promotional Rights

- Viewing

- Equipment Hire

Terms and Conditions

Your name, address and contact details must be printed on your terms and conditions.

Terms and conditions form the contract between you and your customer. Whilst it is your responsibility to complete an order to the specifications agreed, terms and conditions are designed to limit your liability, protect your rights and reduce your exposure to possible loss, but must be fair to both parties. They also set out mutual expectations, which can avoid misunderstandings later. It is important that your customer is aware of, agrees to, and is provided with a copy of any terms and conditions to which their order is subject. They would normally include information about:

- Price
- Deposits
- Payment arrangements
- Alterations
- Specification of order
- Collection, delivery and set-up
- Cancellations and refunds
- Copyright
- Publication and promotional rights
- Viewing
- Equipment hire

The list is not exhaustive and each business should set its own relevant terms and conditions. The form on pages 80 to 81 provides examples of possible terms and conditions for inclusion whilst the following points consider the practicalities and rationale behind them.

Price

The total price of the order needs to be clearly stated. This should include any ancillary costs such as delivery and hire charges. When setting terms and conditions refer to where this information is found (usually the order form and invoice).

Deposits

The minimum amount of deposit taken for any cake order should cover the ingredients and materials needed to complete the cake and is paid when the order is placed. This provides you with some protection should the client cancel or fail to pay. The deposit also 'reserves' the order day allowing you to create a schedule for your other work. The client must be informed of the level of deposit, and whether this is refundable or not. On short-notice cake orders, full payment should be taken upon placement of the order. All deposits taken need to be recorded and a receipt issued. A deposit may not always be taken when the order is placed, e.g. if a client makes an online payment. As soon as the deposit is received, issue a receipt. Only when a deposit is received should the order be deemed accepted.

Payment Arrangements

Clients need to know how payment is to be made, when and where. Offering your clients several ways to pay can increase your business.

Cash payments offer an easy payment method. The usual security measures need to be taken: see how to check a bank note at **www.bankofengland. co.uk/banknotes/current/index.htm**.

Cheques remain an option at the time of writing although are likely to be phased out as soon as 2014. Prior to the release or acceptance of the order, cheques need to be cleared. Be aware of the need to comply with the bank's terms and conditions for accepting cheques. There is a risk that the money may be reclaimed if the cheque turns out to be stolen, fraudulently altered or counterfeit. For any high-value sums alternative means of payment such as cash, internet transfer, phone banking payment, or another secure bank transfer should be considered.

Automated internet or phone payments can be made by individuals or businesses. Banks offering telephone or internet banking services can transfer money directly to another account using the account details of the person or company being paid. You will need to provide the correct sort code and account details to clients plus a reference (such as the order number) so that when you receive monies, it is clear from whom and for what it is received.

The Faster Payments Service (FPS) for telephone and internet payments enables money to be transferred within hours. Using this service means that orders can be processed much quicker.

Credit card/debit card payments will incur a fee so this may not be viable initially for the small business.

For information on website orders and payments please refer to Chapter 9: Websites and E-commerce.

In the case of late payment or payment failure, it is important to advise the limit of your responsibility, the timescale involved and any impact it may have on their order.

Alterations

A request from your customer to alter an existing order may involve additional workload and cost, whilst very late alterations may simply not be possible. However, maintaining a good relationship with the customer is crucial, particularly in a small business. Advise them of the importance of notifying you as soon as possible and that you will do everything to help fulfil their request, but in rare cases this cannot be guaranteed. Inform them of any additional costs before going ahead.

Specifications of the Order

Specifications of the order are the exact order requirements as agreed with the customer for the completion of the commission. Sometimes items forming part of an order are no longer available from your supplier such as decorative pieces, specific colours, stands or other component parts. This is particularly relevant when a wedding order is taken some 18 months or more in advance. You may wish to advise of this possibility and the procedure for progress.

Collection Delivery, and Set-up

If a cake is to be collected from you, advise collection times and whether an appointment is needed. As a sole trader it may be useful to limit collections to arranged times only. Remember to obtain a signature from the customer confirming that the cake order is received in good condition.

If the cake is to be collected, you may wish to include a clause stating that your company accepts no responsibility once the cake has left the premises.

If a cake is to be delivered to the customer or to a venue, provide information of available delivery arrangements and times and the need for a signature on delivery confirming receipt of the cake order in good condition. Advise of the procedure in the case of non-delivery, e.g. if the recipient is not in.

If you are delivering and setting up a cake to a wedding or party venue, advise the customer that venue staff will be asked to sign a form confirming receipt of the cake and that this has been set up and left in good condition. It is worthwhile taking a photograph of the cake once set up prior to departure from the venue: this avoids any misunderstanding should the cake become damaged later. Again, you may choose to include a clause stating that your company accepts no responsibility once the cake has been left at the venue.

Cancellation and Refunds

Set out any cancellation charges clearly and any provision for refunds. Because of the nature of the business, it is almost impossible to sell on a cancelled order therefore cancellation charges need to apply. They also need to be realistic to be certain you are not unfairly financially disadvantaged.

You may have invested considerable time and expense in a cancelled order or declined other orders. In many business sectors it is standard practice to stagger the level of cancellation charges according to the nature of the order and time of cancellation. Consider your own preferences and circumstances, explore other cancellation terms and set your own charges accordingly. The client must be fully aware of the terms and conditions applicable before placing an order.

Copyright

Copyright means exclusive ownership of an original work (see page 44), so any designs you create belong to you. You may have spent considerable time creating these designs and you may not wish for others to copy or use those designs. Make it clear if this is the case (an example of wording is given in the example on page 81). Copyright also applies to websites. Designs which are generic would normally not be included in copyright as they are of a very general nature, e.g. a three-tier wedding cake decorated with coloured sugar spots, a chocolate cake with cigarillos and curls, or cupcakes topped with piped buttercream and sugar roses. For more information about copyright visit **www.ipo.gov.uk**.

Publication and Promotional Rights

This covers the instances where you may want to use images of a bespoke cake or design you have created for a client for promotional or marketing purposes, such as in brochures or magazines. Before you use any such material there should be mutual agreement between yourself and the customer. Whilst some customers would be happy for the world to view their cake order, others may not so I would always suggest sensitivity in this area.

Viewing

A condition is sometimes imposed for wedding cake orders to limit the liability of any errors or omissions should viewing of a completed order be declined and a subsequent complaint lodged. In some instances viewing may not be practical and an alternative solution would be to forward an image to the client.

Equipment Hire

A deposit to cover the full replacement cost of equipment hired can be taken to ensure in the case of a non-return a replacement can be made without financial loss. Deposits taken are generally refunded upon safe return of items hired, less a figure if they are damaged. If a customer wishes to hire a particular stand, for example, and you hire this for them from a third party company, in the case of non-return the liability lies with yourself and not the customer as you entered into a contract to hire with the third party. If this situation should arise, you may wish to ask the customer to hire directly from the third party. In addition to a deposit there may also be a hire charge. Notify them of all costs involved and include the necessary paperwork.

The final decision to impose any terms and conditions remains with you. The examples described here give an indication of the possibilities that you may want to consider for inclusion. Select, simplify, reduce or extend any of the examples, or create originals to suit your own business needs. Simplicity and clarity are often the best course. Seeking advice from professionals such as Business Link or a solicitor on the insertion and content of any terms and conditions imposed is often worthwhile, especially where there may be legal implications.

Kathy Moore Cakes

The Bakery House, Beach Road, Sandborough, Lancashire FY8 123
Telephone: +44 (0) 1253 123 456 Email: KathyMooreCakes@Lime.net
Website: www.kathymoorecakes.co.uk

Terms and Conditions of Sale

All sales made by the Company are subject to the following terms and conditions.

Nothing contained within these terms and conditions affects your statutory rights as a consumer. Please read the following terms and conditions: if there is anything you don't understand please feel free to contact us.

Price

The price for the order shall be as stated on your order form. You agree to pay the full price to the Company in accordance with the order form after the details are checked and agreed by you.

Deposits

All wedding cake orders require a non-refundable deposit of 50% of the total cost. All other cake orders require a non-refundable deposit of 25% but not less than £25.00.

Please note that all deposits are non-refundable and non-transferable.

All deposits become due when the order has been placed and details checked and agreed by you. All orders are deemed to have been accepted only when the deposit has been paid.

Payments

Payment may by made by:

Automated payments - Direct Bank/Building Society Transfer
Account: 0123456789
Sort Code: 01.01.01
Reference: Name

Building Society Payment
Cash
Credit/Debit Card

Final payments

Final payments for all orders must be made at least 28 days prior to delivery/collection/set-up or as stated on your order form.

Non-payments

In the event that any payment is subsequently declined, the order will not be completed or released until alternative funding arrangements have been agreed and payment is made in full. Subsequent completion of the order will be subject to availability and cannot be guaranteed. The Company accepts no responsibility for any loss howsoever caused or for non-delivery under these circumstances. The customer will be responsible for the payment of any additional charges which have been incurred as a result of payment failure.

Alterations to orders

Your cake is very important to us. Please take the time to check your copy of the order form carefully and let us know within three days if changes are needed. It is your responsibility to advise the Company of any alterations to the original order. The Company reserves the right to increase a quoted fee in the event that the Customer requests a variation to the work agreed. Whilst every effort will be made to assist Customers, please note that late changes cannot always be guaranteed.

Cake component parts

From time to time certain materials for our celebration cakes and wedding cakes may become obsolete or no longer be available from our suppliers, for example, pre-manufactured items or ribbon colours. This is totally out of our control, however we will we will endeavour to re-design a cake to reflect as closely as possible the original design using replacement products. In all cases we will try to contact you to advise you of any such changes, however the Company reserves the right to replace these with components of equal or better quality without consultation.

Collection

Your order may be collected at a pre-arranged time between Monday and Friday, 9.00a.m. to 5.00p.m. If you wish to collect outside of these times please contact us and we will do our best to help. A signature is required upon collection confirming that you have received your order in good condition and as specified.

Delivery

Your order can be delivered between 9.00a.m. and 5.00p.m. Monday to Friday or 9.00a.m. to 1.00p.m. Saturday unless by prior agreement between you and the Company. All delivery times are subject to availability. If you have a specific delivery date and require delivery before a given time, please specify this when placing your order. We will do our best to accommodate your requirements.

It is the Customer's responsibility to ensure that you have given us correct delivery information, and that someone is available to receive your cake. A signature will be required for the receipt of the order upon delivery.

If the recipient is not in, the order will be returned to the Company who will contact you to arrange an alternative delivery time for which an additional charge will be payable by the customer. The Company accepts no responsibility for any loss or consequential loss incurred by the Customer as a result, e.g. a wedding without a wedding cake.

We are able to offer personal delivery locally. To the remainder of the UK mainland delivery is by courier. In the event that your order is delivered by courier, please check your cakes before signing for them, as once signed for any compensation for damages will have to be claimed from the courier by you.

Setting up

Should you require your cake to be delivered, the Company will deliver and set up your cake as agreed and will want to ensure it is displayed at its best. It is your responsibility to ensure that you have provided the Company with the set-up details and arrangements made with the venue for the location and display of your cake. The Company cannot be held responsible for the location of the cake at the venue. Please ensure, therefore, that the display location is level, stable and strong enough to hold the cake.

Please also remember that chocolate-covered cakes can melt in warm conditions such as inside a marquee on a hot summer's day, or when set up in direct sunlight.

Once the cake has been collected or delivered, set up, and signed for, the Company is unable to accept liability for any interference with or damage to the cake thereafter.

If a cake is to be delivered and set up by the Company, a signature will be required from your venue management confirming the cake has been received and set up in good condition. A photograph of the cake will be taken prior to departure by the Company to verify that the cake has been set up and left in good condition.

Cancellations/refunds

Wedding cake or special order cancellations:
As your wedding cake and/or special order booking is reserved solely for you and certain components for your cake/s may be ordered months in advance, the following conditions are implemented when an order is cancelled:

6 months from delivery date - 50% of the total cost will be payable.

0 to 3 months from delivery date - 100% of the total cost will be payable.

Wedding cake/special order cancellations must be made in writing.

Other cake order cancellations:
Full payment is required if cancellation is within 2 months of delivery date, prior to this a refund of any monies paid, less deposit, will be made.

Copyright

Please note that no person shall have entitlement to copy or reproduce in any form, or otherwise make use of any image, photograph, design or other document or item produced by or on behalf of the Company without the prior written consent of the Company.

Publication and promotional rights

By signing the Order Form the Customer agrees that the Company is the sole designer and owner of the final cake design. All rights in any original designs created and designed by the Company shall remain the exclusive property of the Company. From time to time our designs are published in the media, e.g. wedding magazines. We reserve the right to use any image of a Customer's cake made by the Company for publication after the delivery date unless previously agreed in writing between the Customer and the Company.

The Customer has no ownership rights over any cake design. Exclusivity of cake designs between our Customers is not guaranteed unless the Customer commissions an exclusive design.

Viewing

Please note cakes with sponge tiers/cupcakes may not be completed until the day prior to or the day of the celebration to ensure the cakes are as fresh as possible. Please prearrange viewings of any wedding cakes ordered. The Company accepts no liability for any omissions or errors on wedding cakes if they are not viewed by the Customer prior to the wedding.

Allergies

Please be aware that whilst your chosen cake may not be made with nuts or a nut product, it will be prepared in a kitchen where nut products may be used in other cakes and fillings. Raw materials used may not be free from dairy, wheat or gluten. Allergy information is provided with all cake orders.

- Content
- Design
- Quality
- Image

Brochures and Price Lists

The brochure you create will identify you and your business. It can be used to great advantage as an effective and powerful marketing tool and will play an important role in the success of your business. Having chosen your pricing structure for your cakes (see Chapter 4), the choice of content and design will be crucial in projecting the right image to tempt and tantalise your target market and illustrate how your business meets their needs. You want potential customers to pick up your brochure in preference to others, so how can this be achieved?

The content and design need to generate interest, and be informative, clear, attractive and appealing. The objectives of a brochure are:

- to tempt people to open your brochure and learn more.

- to arouse curiosity and a desire for your product.

- to get the right message across.

Content

Contact details

A brochure should let potential customers know where you are and how you can be contacted. Details would normally include:

- Business name

- Business address

- Telephone/fax number

- Email address

- Website address

- Hours of business

Remember, you are required to show clearly on the appropriate forms your business name and contact

details in order to comply with the Companies Act 2006 (see Chapter 2: The Business Plan). Consider the personal information you print on your brochure and whether you want your home address shown: in some instances a contact telephone number, email address or website is all that is required. If the brochures are to be left in public places, consider your security and privacy at home before giving out personal details.

Your products and services

Potential customers need to know what your business can offer and how it can meet their needs.

- Decide what information you want to include: keep it clear and concise and word it appropriately. Never use jargon.

- Include a 'key message', that is, the most important thing you want to convey to your customers.

- Include details of your business: provide information about the variety of cakes available such as wedding, celebration, corporate, novelty, baby shower, themed cakes, cupcakes, mini cakes, whoopie pies and decorated cookies.

- Describe the service you can offer: personal attention, flexibility, planning and design, consultations, delivery, co-ordinating ancillary items, equipment hire and set up.

- Draw attention to the benefits your business can provide: individual design planning or pre-designed ranges; modern, traditional and fun designs; a wide range of homemade cake bases; mix and match recipe options; specialist choices such as organic, vegetarian or gluten-free cakes.

- Provide information on prices: this can be included in the brochure or detailed on a separate list which can be used independently or in conjunction with the brochure. Be certain it is quite clear exactly what is included in the price.

Remember that all the details you give must be accurate. Make sure you can support any claim you make about your business, products or services (see Trading Standards on page 42).

Design

As well as being informative, your brochure needs to be attractive, appealing and tempting! Image is important and first impressions count. When designing your brochure, consider the image you want to create, the market you want to target and the business you want to attract.

- Choose a colour scheme.

- Consider layout, size and functionality: look at tri-fold brochures, book fold brochures, double-sided glossy brochures, four-fold brochures and other samples to see which layout you prefer.

- Create interest and attract attention by using an imaginative design that reflects your business image and style.

- Explore and use an appropriate font with generous line spacing to create text that is easy and clear to read.

- Review and update images or graphics to ensure they reflect current or future market trends.

- Remember that simplicity is often the best choice of design.

If you are not confident at designing your own brochure, there are graphic design companies who offer this service. Make sure you include any costs in your business plan (see pages 16 to 29).

Quality

Whether you have chosen to create the brochure design yourself or elected to use a design service, the choice and quality of printing material plays a key role in the projection of a professional, high standard business operation.

I would always advise that you use the best quality printing paper and card that is within your budget. Investigate the ranges of specialised paper and card available from suppliers and choose the weight, feel, texture and colour to suit your business and your business image.

Image

The same information presented with different artwork can portray very different images: the samples on the following pages provide the same information but each has a very different image. Consider your potential customers and future opportunities when deciding on your business image.

Once you have created your brochure consider using some part of the design or your logo on all other business stationery to achieve a co-ordinated and professional image (see Chapter 5). As with your brochure, use the best quality paper and card available, especially when printing your own stationery.

Remember copyright law. If you are using any graphics, images, logos or other pictures, use only your own designs or those you have proper entitlement to use.

Creating your own brochure will be the start of planning your marketing strategy: information about marketing and advertising your business is given in the next chapter.

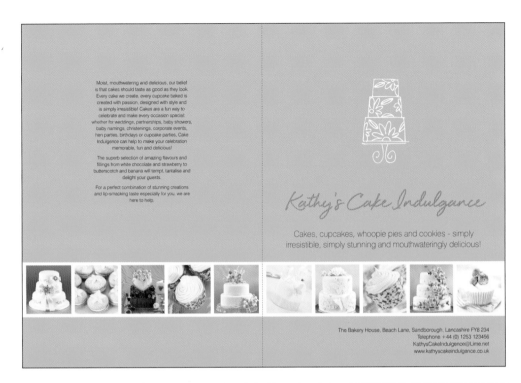

Moist, mouthwatering and delicious, our belief is that cakes should taste as good as they look. Every cake we create, every cupcake baked is created with passion, designed with style and is simply irresistible! Cakes are a fun way to celebrate and make every occasion special: whether for weddings, partnerships, baby showers, baby namings, christenings, corporate events, hen parties, birthdays or cupcake parties, Cake Indulgence can help to make your celebration memorable, fun and delicious!

The superb selection of amazing flavours and fillings from white chocolate and strawberry to butterscotch and banana will tempt, tantalise and delight your guests.

For a perfect combination of stunning creations and lip-smacking taste especially for you, we are here to help.

Kathy's Cake Indulgence

Cakes, cupcakes, whoopie pies and cookies - simply irresistible, simply stunning and mouthwateringly delicious!

The Bakery House, Beach Lane, Sandborough, Lancashire FY8 234
Telephone +44 (0) 1253 123456
KathysCakeIndulgence@Lime.net
www.kathyscakeindulgence.co.uk

Monstrous, massive and amazing!!

Designed to thrill! Our cakes take on the most amazing shapes, from the simplest of cupcakes to a tower of sculptured cake art! It does not stop there — we believe our cakes should taste as amazing as they look and we hand bake each one. The range of flavours and fillings is impressive so there is something for everyone, something different to tempt, tantalise and excite your guests! A cake makes every occasion special, and Cake Indulgence is delighted to be able to help make your occasion memorable and fun. Whether your celebration is a wedding, civil partnership, birthday, baby shower, hen party or a corporate event, indulge yourself and your guests with one of our amazing cakes!

The Bakery House,
Beach Lane,
Sandborough,
Lancashire
FY8 234
Telephone +44 (0) 1253 123456
KathysCakeIndulgence@Lime.net
www.kathyscakeindulgence.co.uk

Kathy's Cake Indulgence!

FABULOUS, FANTASTIC AND FUN!

www.kathyscakeindulgence.co.uk

The Bakery House, Beach Lane, Sandborough, Lancashire FY8 234
Telephone +44 (0) 1253 123456
KathysCakeIndulgence@Lime.net
www.kathyscakeindulgence.co.uk

'Moist, mouthwatering and delicious, our belief is that cakes should taste as good as they look. Every cake we create, every cupcake baked is created with passion, designed with style and is simply irresistible! Cakes are a fun way to celebrate and make every occasion special: whether for weddings, partnerships, baby showers, baby namings, christenings, corporate events, hen parties, birthdays or cupcake parties, Cake Indulgence can help to make your celebration memorable, fun and delicious!

The superb selection of amazing flavours and fillings from white chocolate and strawberry to butterscotch and banana will tempt, tantalise and delight your guests.

For a perfect combination of stunning creations and lip-smacking taste especially for you, we are here to help.

Kathy's Cake Indulgence

Fabulous, fun and frivolous!

Kathy's Cake Indulgence
The Bakery House, Beach Lane, Sandborough, Lancashire FY8 234.
Telephone +44 (0) 1253 123456
KathysCakeIndulgence@Lime.net
www.kathyscakeindulgence.co.uk

The Bakery House, Beach Lane,
Sandborough, Lancashire FY8 234
Telephone +44 (0) 1253 123456
KathysCakeIndulgence@Lime.net
www.kathyscakeindulgence.co.uk

Moist, mouthwatering and delicious, our belief is that cakes should taste as good as they look. Every cake we create, every cupcake baked is created with passion, designed with style and is simply irresistible! Cakes are a fun way to celebrate and make every occasion special: whether for weddings, partnerships, baby showers, baby namings, christenings, corporate events, hen parties, birthdays or cupcake parties, Cake Indulgence can help to make your celebration memorable, fun and delicious!

The superb selection of amazing flavours and fillings from white chocolate and strawberry to butterscotch and banana will tempt, tantalise and delight your guests.

For a perfect combination of stunning creations and lip-smacking taste especially for you, we are here to help.

Created with passion, finished with style - simply must-have cakes!

The Bakery House, Beach Lane, Sandborough, Lancashire FY8 234.
Telephone +44 (0) 1253 123456
KathysCakeIndulgence@Lime.net
www.kathyscakeindulgence.co.uk

Kathy's Cake Indulgence

Irresistible, individual and indulgent!

Fabulous, fun and frivolous!

The Bakery House, Beach Lane,
Sandborough, Lancashire FY8 234
Telephone +44 (0) 1253 123456
KathysCakeIndulgence@Lime.net
www.kathyscakeindulgence.co.uk

Kathy's Cake Indulgence

- Marketing

- Advertising Material

- Training

Marketing and Advertising your Business

If you get enough business through recommendations and word of mouth, you may not need to market or advertise. However, with changing economic climates and market trends it would be prudent to be aware of – and identify at an early stage – options available for new and future business opportunities. Each business will be different but the one common denominator is the need for a continuous source of custom and there are several methods that can help you achieve this for your business.

You won't sell anything to anyone if your customers don't know you are there!

Marketing

Once you have identified your target markets (see Markets on page 23) you need to have a strategy that will enable you to communicate the benefits of what your business offers to your potential customers. A marketing plan should always be realistic, achievable, cost- and time-effective and designed to suit your own business needs.

Meeting people

Meeting people has many advantages – it is personal and you can answer any questions that the enquirer may have. It gives you the chance to build relationships with potential clients whom you may meet through friends or contacts.

Word of mouth

This is one of the best forms of advertising so make certain you achieve and maintain a reputation for high standards, service and outstanding customer satisfaction – all of which are

central to the concept of a good marketing. Let all your friends, colleagues and associates know of your new business venture.

Local groups, schools and colleges

'Spreading the word' is an excellent way to promote your business. Many local groups are looking for a guest speaker and combined with a cake display, images or even a short demonstration, giving a talk or demonstration allows you to meet customers face to face and sell your business. Have plenty of brochures and business cards with you and always take an appointment book. Try to identify the groups as being within your target market with potential custom.

Wedding exhibitions

If one of your target markets is brides-to-be then wedding exhibitions are an ideal way to reach a core group. The charges for exhibiting vary considerably and a firm quote should be obtained specifying exactly what is included. If you do decide to take a stand, plan a cake display which is not overly fussy and includes wedding cakes of varied designs, styles and trends. Display them imaginatively to give the 'wow' factor. If you have the opportunity to select your stand location, choose one with plenty of light, in a prominent position and which catches trade both inward and outward. Cakes and cupcakes in different designs ensure you attract not only the wedding market but other potential clients for celebration, corporate or children's cakes. You may wish to offer cake samples, in which case mini cupcakes are attractive (make sure you include this in your costs).

If you are starting your business on a relatively small scale, taking a stand at an exhibition may not be right for you. Being inundated with order requests is one thing, completing them all is another. You need to be realistic about how much work you can take on. If you decide that you aren't ready to exhibit, visiting wedding exhibitions is an excellent way to do some market research.

Local hotels, restaurants and wedding venues

Wherever there are venues for weddings, hen parties, birthdays or any celebration, make contact and find out if there is an opening for you. Take images, advertising material and business cards with you.

Local trade fairs

See who is offering what and identify additional opportunities for your own business. Talk to the traders, exchange business cards and get to know local businesses. Often you can help each other out.

Local community events

Community events present opportunites as either a networking exercise or for hands-on involvement. Be aware of future planned events which could require your services.

New parent/parent and toddler groups

Catch the market from day one! Cakes and cupcakes are often made to celebrate baby showers, new babies, baby naming and christenings and future business opportunities are huge. Leaflets, brochures and personal appearances could bring in a large and potentially ongoing business market.

Making contacts

Approach local businesses as they may be willing to promote your new business.

Local radio, television and newspapers/bulletins/magazines

Make contact with local radio and television production teams. Advertising costs in these sectors would usually be well above most budgets, but local interest broadcasts are popular and they may be interested in doing a short feature with you, especially if you have some fabulous cakes to show or a story to tell.

Shop links

Associated businesses may be willing to display your cakes in spare window space, particularly during seasonal or themed periods. Photographers, event management companies, florists, jewellers and baby shops may all be willing to develop a relationship with your business for mutual benefit.

Corporate and sporting events

Local company events, grand openings, anniversaries and other celebrations are all opportunities for you to make contact with corporate clients and to let them know of the benefits your business can offer. Make their business yours. Similarly, sporting events are a good opportunity for you to offer your business services to local clubs.

Websites

Websites have the potential to reach a wide target market with little effort so it pays to have a presence on other sites (you may opt for a reciprocal link for mutual benefit). Be certain your geographic limitations are detailed and that any images you use are of the best possible quality. You need to comply with all necessary legislation if you are advertising or selling online (see Chapter 9: Websites and E-commerce).

Create interest

Creating interest in your product is the first step to selling your products and services.

Create a portfolio

One of the best ways of attracting customers is to let them see your work. Create a professionally presented portfolio of your own work and, if possible, have this available as a digital file so that you can save it and take it anywhere with you. Use your images on advertising material, brochures and leaflets. Consider launching your own website (see page 96).

Put yourself on the map

Be sure people know how to contact you and when. Offer more than one contact choice to make it easy for potential customers.

Build up the right image and reputation

Maintain style, quality and customer service in all your business dealings.

There are many marketing methods in addition to the ones discussed above, e.g. e-marketing, but only those most relevant to the purposes of this book have been included here.

For any marketing activity, look at the possible costs involved as well as the level of time and commitment required. Balance this against the level of potential financial return in the short and medium term before deciding on the most appropriate and effective marketing activity for your business.

Formulate a list of marketing activities which will ensure you reach your target customers, make contact with them and create interest. You need to communicate to them about the products and services you can offer, and how these meet their needs. Your marketing methods may be very diverse depending on your product range.

When you have decided upon your marketing strategy and selected appropriate (if any) marketing activities, developing advertising material to create the right image and create interest is equally as important.

Although marketing is all about generating business, always remember to nurture existing clients!

Advertising Material

Advertising materials can be an excellent resource for building up awareness of your company but they need to be effective, give the right image and get the right message across to the right target market. First impressions count and you want your customers to remember you, know where to contact you and be aware of what you can offer.

- Take time to plan; different marketing activities may require different advertising materials.

- Using your business logo across the whole range of stationery and advertising material creates a uniform and professional appearance.

- Labels are easy to produce and can be used on cake boxes, letters and parcels. Choose designs and wording that reflect the full extent of your business e.g. say that you make large cakes as well as cupcakes.

Advertising material needs to:

Grab attention

Create interest

Arouse desire

There are several ways in which you can achieve this:

- Make it easy to read with a clear font style and appropriate line spacing.

- Use clear, professional-standard images.

- Use the right information for your target market.

- Provide a choice of contact details for clients – make it easy for them.

- Use appealing and interesting content but keep it simple.

- Identify the benefits and features of your business.

- Identify your unique selling points.

- Project a key message.

As a sole trader working from home consider the extent of contact details you want to publish on any advertising material purely from a security point of view. On the relevant business stationery, your address is compulsory (see pages 64 to 65).

Carry business cards with you wherever you go and ask if you can leave leaflets in waiting rooms, hairdressers, nail salons, fabric shops, stationers, party shops, bridal outfitters, event management shops or other local places where there is the possibility of reaching your target market.

Be aware of changing market trends and fashions. Tailor your advertising to suit your needs, the image you want to create and the customers you want to attract.

Determine what advertising materials are needed for each activity to let potential customers know who you are, where you are, what you can do and the benefits to them. Make sure you include all advertising and marketing costs in your business plan.

Training

Marketing, advertising and selling skills are an important element in any successful business. Being skilled in these areas offers increased business opportunities and greater market leadership - people will remember you for the right reasons. If there are areas you feel less competent in, training is readily available, often without charge, and is a worthwhile investment of your time. Be creative and enjoy! Techniques, hints, tips, guidelines, principles, even the psychology behind marketing, advertising and selling can all be learnt. Contact Business Link (see Useful Contacts, page 106), look at your local college prospectus or search the internet for training resources.

Remember - one of the best forms of advertising is a satisfied customer!

- Creating your own Website

- Distance Selling, E-commerce and the Law

- Website Terms and Conditions

Websites and E-commerce

Creating your own Website

A website can be an excellent channel for promoting your business and the benefits are many:

- Potential customers can look at your 'shop window' at any time and from any location.

- It is a means to advertise your products and services.

- You can highlight the benefits and features of your business.

- Multiple images of your work can be viewed in one place.

- It gives you the opportunity to be interactive with your customers.

- You have the option to trade online.

However, a website will not be suited to every business: whether or not it is potentially useful is often dependent on the size and extent of your company. Before embarking on the creation of a website, first consider how or if your business will benefit. Take into account current business levels and expected future business levels. Do you want, and would you be able to cope with, any extra market demand? How would you maintain the site? Would there be a financial outlay?

If you feel that you want to go ahead with the launch of your own website, plan and design it carefully. When choosing a business name, use a search engine and check if the same domain name is available e.g. Kathy Moore Cakes could be www.kathymoorecakes.co.uk.

What makes a good website	
Simple and clear presentation	Cramming too much onto any page causes confusion and makes the information difficult to read. Keep each page simple and accessible.
Good design	Keep a good overall balance between graphics and text.
Easy to read	Use a clear font style, appropriate line spacing, and keep a strong contrast between text and background for easy reading.
Colour balance	Be consistent in the colours that you use: choose a theme to match your logo.
Effective graphic design	Poor image quality may suggest unprofessional standards. Always use good quality images that portray your work in the best light.
Informative	Information should always be up to date, clear to understand and interesting.
Easy navigation	Pages should be well organised for visitors to navigate with ease. Your homepage, company information, products, services and contact details should be presented in a logical order.
User friendly	The way you organise your site should allow visitors to find what they are looking for quickly and easily.
Appealing and inviting	Make your site visually attractive, creative and tempting!

A well-designed and maintained website can be an excellent marketing tool but it is paramount that the content is up to date and any change in market trends and fashions are reflected. Perhaps most important of all is that people can find your website. Once your website has been built, be certain to check it thoroughly before going live. Ask the opinions of family, friends and colleagues.

You can create your own website online, or use a company to do the work for you. Free programs for building websites are available online or if you want to create the whole site yourself, courses are available both online and at adult education centres. Further advice is given on the Business Link website, **www.businesslink.gov.uk**.

Distance Selling, E-commerce and the Law

An e-commerce business is a business that advertises or sells goods or services online.

Initially you may consider a website, purely for advertising purposes, excluding online selling facilities. The purpose of your website will dictate the level of legislative compliance: it is important to be clear which regulations you need to comply with. In general, if you are not selling, these will include:

- The Privacy and Electronic Communications Regulations 2003

- Data Protection Act 1998

- The Consumer Protection from Unfair Trading Regulations 2008

- Trading Standards

If you are selling then additional compliance will be required with:

- Consumer Protection (Distance Selling) Regulations 2000

- The Electronic Commerce (EC Directive) Regulations 2002

Regulations affecting e-commerce are administered by organisations including Trading Standards, the Office of Fair Trading (OFT) and the Information Commissioner's Office (ICO).

Your website will need to comply with all current regulations and legislation. The purpose of the legislation is to:

- Give consumers the confidence and protection to buy products and services where there is no face-to-face contact with the seller.

- Make certain that any trader selling at a distance meets certain basic requirements and obligations.

The main areas for compliance are:

- Consumer Protection (Distance Selling) Regulations 2000

- The Electronic Commerce (EC Directive) Regulations 2002

- Data Protection Act 1998

- The Privacy and Electronics Communications Regulations 2003

Full details of these can be found at **www.oft.gov.uk**, **www.legislation.gov.uk** and **www.ico.gov.uk**. A useful download entitled Home Shopping - A Guide for Businesses on Distance Selling can be downloaded from the Office of Fair Trading website.

These may seem overwhelming for any small business, but there is plenty of help available. Some of the legislation is very similar to that required for selling direct to the consumer and will therefore be familiar to you. Contact Business Link, which has excellent information sheets on the above (see Useful Contacts on page 106), or download the relevant details from the above websites. Brief notes from each of these regulations are outlined below.

Consumer Protection (Distance Selling) Regulations 2000

If you sell to consumers online, or sell at a distance by another method such as digital TV, mail order, phone or fax, the Distance Selling Regulations apply to you. There are some exceptions to the regulations which are particularly relevant to those running a cake decorating business from home, including cancellation rights. As food is deemed to be non-returnable because of the perishable nature of the product the right to cancel is not enforced.

The key features of the regulations require you to:

- Provide potential customers with specific information in advance, such as your name and address, the products you are selling and the services you are providing, the full price, payment methods, delivery charges, delivery arrangements, and the customers' right to cancel. Your address must be a geographic address: a PO box will generally not suffice.

- Present all information in a clear and easily accessible form.

- Send customers an order confirmation giving information such as your postal address and cancellation arrangements.

The Electronic Commerce (EC Directive) Regulations 2002

These regulations cover the information that online service providers are required to give consumers, particularly how contracts are formed and completed, how terms and conditions are applied, the ordering process and the obligations that sellers must abide by. Some of the legislation overlaps with the Distance Selling Regulations.

The Consumer Protection from Unfair Trading Regulations 2008

This protects consumers from unfair trading practices, including misleading information, actions and omissions.

Data Protection Act 1998

This covers the privacy of the customer and its purpose is to protect the rights of a consumer (or individual) about whom data may be stored, processed and used by controlling the administration and use of the information supplied (see Chapter 3: Formalities and Procedures). It applies to all data, however held. Basically you need to keep any information about your customers secure and confidential and not use this information for any other purposes without their agreement.

The Privacy and Electronics Communications Regulations 2003

This covers marketing by electronic means. If you wish to contact potential or existing customers via electronic marketing methods, and/or you use cookies on your website, you need to comply with the regulations. Visit **www.ico.gov.uk** for further details.

Website Terms and Conditions

If you have a website you may be required to have a set of terms and conditions. These will vary depending on the purpose of your website, i.e. whether you are selling via your site or not. These may include, but are not limited to:

- Your full business name and contact details

- A privacy policy

- A copyright notice covering including images, trademarks and logos

- Security of information

- Website detail changes

- Costs

- Payment options

- Terms and conditions relating to payment

- Delivery policies and charges

- Cancellation rights and refunds policy

- A disclaimer relating to faulty products

Contact Business Link or Lawyers for your Business to confirm the appropriate terms and conditions required for your website.

For information regarding general terms and conditions for your business, please see Chapter 6, pages 74 to 81.

Over the years the way in which we shop has changed dramatically, from pen and quill right through to smart phones and apps! Decide what is best for your current business needs and build this into your business plan. Ensure you budget for upgrades which will be needed as your business grows and as technology advances. Do not be tempted to get carried away at the beginning: gradual development in any business is one of the keys to success and the reason why a business plan is reviewed regularly. A website may not be suitable now, but may be in the future.

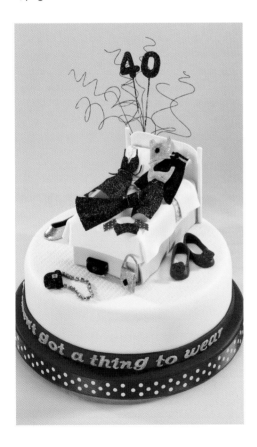

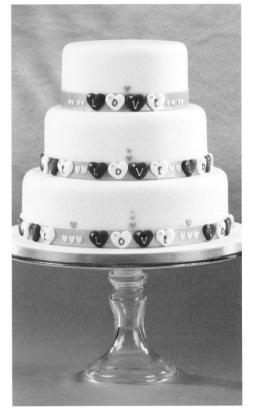

Using Time Effectively

- 20 Ways to Manage your Time

- Making Sugar Decorations

- Assembling Cakes

- Coping with Mistakes

- And Finally...

Time cannot be saved, it can only be used. Using time effectively is an asset to your business whilst poor time management robs your business of profit and compromises a healthy lifestyle balance between business and pleasure.

20 Ways to Manage your Time

1   Record how you currently use your time over a period and analyse it.

2   Use your willpower and learn to be disciplined.

3   Plan a work schedule and write it in a diary or wall planner.

4   Produce a daily task list and keep to it.

5   Arrange to order materials and ingredients in advance so they are ready when you need them.

6   Consider having goods delivered to you.

7   Plan realistic and achievable time estimates.

8   Train – skills and experience give you the knowledge to complete a task efficiently.

9   Learn to say 'no' gracioiusly.

10 Don't procrastinate; anticipate known deadlines.

11 Prioritise – tackle priority jobs first, not those you most enjoy!

12 Allow for interruptions but try to keep them short.

13 If you do get interrupted, get back on track immediately afterwards – don't get further distracted.

14 Reorganise your work area so everything is to hand.

15 Put things back where they belong to avoid spending time searching for them!

16 Organise batch baking whenever you can.

17 Group similar decorations for different jobs and work on them simultaneously whenever possible.

18 Take scheduled breaks during work time to recharge your batteries.

19 Allocate leisure time.

20 Try to arrange clients' appointments in a block.

Recording your planned work and leisure activities either in a diary, wall chart or similar is a very effective way to manage time. You can see at a glance exactly what your commitments are and when. Block off holiday time and schedule in your personal commitments.

Try arranging client appointments/collections on your preferred days to allow you an uninterrupted workflow. Haphazard appointments may be difficult to manage when decorating or baking cakes.

Making Sugar Decorations

Making decorations can be time-consuming. Following these tips will help to save time and avoid last-minute panics.

1 Look at your weekly/fortnightly/monthly sales orders, or as appropriate and identify and record any off-pieces of decoration. Group those of the same types and make them all at the same time.

2 Get out all the equipment, tools and materials you need before you start.

3 Make up any modelling pastes/pastillage the day before to allow ingredients and colours to blend fully.

4 Start with any decorations that are dependent upon drying before subsequent layers/component parts can be attached.

5 When making flowers or leaves, consider their size: larger ones fill more space on a cake, take just the same amount of time to make and are often less fiddly.

6 When attaching florist wires to flower paste, heat the end of the wire over a tea light or similar before inserting into the paste. The wire will stick instantly as it is burnt into the sugar, allowing you to work immediately on soft paste without the wire becoming dislodged. Do be careful as the wires get very hot!

7 Make the most of greenery: for unspecified filler greenery use the same leaf shape with a different veiner, paste colour and shading.

8 To speed up drying time of decorations such as figures and flowers, work under an angleposie lamp: it is easier on the eyes too! You can also hang wired items such as leaves from empty radiator towel rails and place decorations in the airing cupboard to dry.

9 Avoid making sugar figures or any off-pieces of decoration in a damp atmosphere; paste, particularly coloured paste, can become sticky, difficult to work with and take a disproportionate amount of time to dry. Consider purchasing a dehumidifier if the problem is persistent.

10 Steam multiple wired leaves and flowers by securing a whole batch in a polystyrene block and passing through the steam in one go.

11 Try to dust/paint all objects at the same time.

12 If you need strongly coloured modelling paste/flower paste/sugarpaste, buy commercially made coloured paste rather than make your own. Adding large amounts of colouring to obtain strong colours can change both the consistency and properties of the paste and can prolong drying times.

13 When using edible glitter, place objects on a large piece of kitchen roll which can then be folded over, and the excess glitter returned to the pot without the need to clear down a whole worktop.

Assembling Cakes

1   When assembling delicate sprays or other decorations, work over a large piece of sponge so if you drop anything, there is less chance of it breaking.

2   When making up flower sprays, leave space for an imaginary butterfly to flit between leaves and petals. An overcrowded arrangement can look heavy and unnatural and take up excessive time. Look at the natural gaps in real bushes and shrubs and mimic this in your sugar sprays.

3   It is of prime importance that cakes are dowelled correctly to avoid accidents and time consuming corrective measures, including your reputation! Allow plenty of time to dowel your cakes and measure the correct distance between dowels to provide the stability needed. Cakes are often set up many hours before being disassembled for cutting and need to have the stability to withstand this (and the occasional accidental knock from passing guests!). Detailed instructions, templates and patterns can be found in my first book, *Cakes from Concept to Creation*, published by B. Dutton Publishing (see jacket).

Coping with Mistakes

Any successful business needs to aim for and maintain the highest possible standards of quality, service and reputation. However, occasional small mistakes will happen now and then so don't worry when they do – you may be able to save the situation! The odd small blemish may seem like disaster but remember:

- There is always a front and a back to any cake.

- Blemishes disappear when a decoration is placed appropriately.

- You can add character to your work with a little extra touch such as a ladybird; they are also ideal for covering small flaws.

And Finally...

You are your business. All the planning, preparation and organisation will have been time well spent to give your business the best chance of success. Nearly all successful businesses are built on someone's passion: the passion that brings enjoyment in wanting to offer your best, that gives you the drive to achieve the highest possible standards and the desire to develop that into a flourishing and rewarding business. All that needs to be done now is for me to wish you well, to wish you success and most of all to wish you enjoyment.

Useful Contacts

The British Sugarcraft Guild

www.bsguk.org

national office@bsguk.org

020 8859 6943

A national guild providing members with the latest sugarcraft news and events. Local branches all over the UK hold exhibitions, competitions and other events for sugarcrafters in each region.

Business Gateway (Scotland)

www.bgateway.com

0845 609 6611

Business Link (UK)

www.businesslink.gov.uk

0845 600 9 006

Objective information, support and advice for those setting up and in business with local operators throughout England. Find your nearest Business Link online.

Companies House

www.companies-house.gov.uk

0303 1234 500

The organisation which holds information about limited companies in the UK and makes it accessible to the public, including usage of business names and the requirements of the Companies Act 2006.

Culpitt Ltd.

www.culpitt.com

info@culpitt.com

01670 814545

Supplier of cake and food decorating products and equipment to the trade.

Flexible Support for Business (Wales)

www.business.wales.gov.uk

businesssupport@wales.gsi.gov.uk

03000 6 03000

Food Standards Agency

www.food.gov.uk

www.sfbbtraining.co.uk

helpline@foodstandards.gsi.gov.uk

020 7276 8829 (UK office)

01224 285100 (Scotland)

02920 678999 (Wales)

028 9041 7700 (Northern Ireland)

Guy, Paul & Co. Ltd.

www.guypaul.co.uk

sales@guypaul.co.uk

01494 432121

Supplier of sugarcraft and bakery items to the trade.

Health & Safety Executive

www.hse.gov.uk

0845 345 0055

HM Revenue & Customs

www.hmrc.gov.uk

0845 300 0627

Information and servies for starting up in business, including tax issues, National Insurance and evaluation reports.

Information Commissioner's Office

www.ico.gov.uk

0303 123 1113

Provides information about data protection, including the Data Protection Act 1998.

Invest Northern Ireland

www.nibusinessinfo.co.uk

0800 027 0639

Intellectual Property Office

www.ipo.gov.uk

information@ipo.gov.uk

0300 300 2000

The Law Society

www.lawsociety.org.uk

020 7242 1222

Offers advice on legal matters, including a list of participating members in the Lawyers for your Business scheme.

Learn Direct

www.learndirect.co.uk

0800 101 901

Online training and local centres offering courses on all aspects of training, plus impartial information on adult learning courses throughout the UK.

National Business Register LLP

www.start.biz

sales@start.biz

0121 678 9000

Provides information on registered business names and domain names and offers a free online name search.

Office of Fair Trading

www.oft.gov.uk

enquiries@oft.gsi.gov.uk

08454 04 05 06

Office of Public Sector Information

www.opsi.gov.uk

www.legislation.gov.uk

Provides information about the latest government legislation, including health and safety and data protection.

Orchard Products

www.orchardproducts.co.uk

01273 419418

Manufacturer and supplier of fine quality sugarcraft cutters and tools. Shop and mail order.

Smeg UK Ltd.

www.smeguk.com

www.smegretro.co.uk

Italian appliance manufacturer Smeg produces distinctive domestic appliances combining design, performance and quality.

Squires Kitchen

www.squires-shop.com

www.squires-school.co.uk

customer@squires-shop.com

0845 61 71 810

Supplier of sugarcraft colours, tools, equipment, marzipan and icings; publisher of sugarcraft books and magazines; international school of cake decorating and sugarcraft. Shop, online shop and mail order service.

The Stationery Office

www.tso.co.uk

0870 600 5522

customer.services@tso.co.uk

A bookshop where hundreds of thousands of titles are available, including government legislation and regulations.

Trading Standards

www.tradingstandards.gov.uk

membership@tsi.org.uk

0845 608 9428

Provides information on consumer protection in the UK. The website provides contact details for your local Trading Standards Office.

UK Fire Service Resources

www.fireservice.co.uk

www.avonfire.gov.uk

SQUIRES KITCHEN
International School

The confidence to create

At Squires Kitchen, we believe anyone can bake beautifully, master the art of cake decorating and sugarcraft and make chocolates like a professional; all you need is confidence.

Whether you're a beginner, a home cake maker or a professional pastry chef there's a course to suit you, from covering a cake with icing to creating chocolate centrepieces.

Whilst we offer a professional service, it's our family feel and homely approach that keep students coming back to Squires Kitchen's school time and time again. We've inspired many sugarcrafters, bakers and cake decorators who came to learn with us and have now gone on to be very successful in their fields.

Sugarcraft

Learn everything from covering a cake to piping, modelling and making sugar flowers.

Chocolate

Discover how to make chocolates, desserts and cakes like the professionals.

Cookery

Become a domestic god or goddess by learning how to make delicious cakes, biscuits, speciality breads and pastries.

'Very good facilities. Very relaxed and friendly atmosphere. We covered many areas of chocolate uses; I learnt a large amount to detailed information on chocolate.'

"Each technique was explained and demonstrated clearly, making you feel confident upon doing it yourself.'

The new purpose-built room was very comfortable, had good light and lots of relevant equipment.'

We work with a fabulous team of regular tutors who are the very best in their specialist areas, ensuring you get expert guidance every step of the way. Not only are they great teachers, they are lovely people who will share with you their vast experience and tricks of the trade, giving you the confidence to bake, make and decorate like a professional.

We also feature guest tutors on a regular basis, so please do check our website or give us a call if you are looking for someone specific.

The right course for you is just a click or a call away! Visit **www.squires-school.co.uk** or call **0845 61 71 810**.

FOR MORE INFORMATION:

Contact the Course Co-ordinator at Squires Kitchen International School of Cake Decorating and Sugarcraft, The Grange, Hones Yard, Farnham, Surrey, GU9 8BB, UK. Tel: 0845 61 71 810 (UK, local call charges apply), +44 (0)1252 260 260 (outside UK). See our full course list and book courses online at **www.squires-school.co.uk**.

Notes

Notes